To Tell at Last

Blanca

TO TELL AT LAST

Survival under False Identity, 1941–45

BLANCA ROSENBERG

UNIVERSITY OF ILLINOIS PRESS

Urbana and Chicago

This book was published with the support of the Jacob and Clara Egit Foundation for Holocaust and Jewish Resistance Literature, Toronto, Canada, through the Histadrut Assistance Fund.

Illini Books edition, 1995
© 1993 by the Board of Trustees of the University of Illinois
Manufactured in the United States of America
1 2 3 4 5 C P 5 4 3 2 1

This book is printed on acid-free paper.

Library of Congress Cataloging-in-Publication Data

Rosenberg, Blanca
    To tell at last : survival under false identity, 1941–45 / Blanca
Rosenberg.
        p.   cm.
    Includes index.
    ISBN 0-252-01998-9 (alk. paper). — ISBN 0-252-06391-0 (pbk. :
alk. paper)
        1. Rosenberg, Blanca, 1913–   . 2. Jews—Poland—Biography.
    3. Holocaust, Jewish (1939–1945)—Poland—Personal narratives.
    4. Poland—Biography. I. Title.
    DS135.P63R66957   1993
    940.53'18'09438092—dc20
    [B]   92-32695
                                                       CIP

If thou didst ever hold me in thy heart,
Absent thee from felicity awhile,
And in this harsh world draw thy breath in pain
To tell my story.

Hamlet

*To the memory of all my dear and loved ones and to my children,
Alex, Mark, and Merle, and grandchildren,
Adrianne and Eugene*

Contents

Photographs follow p. 38.

Acknowledgments

Many people helped me to tell my story.

My first and very special thanks go to my son Alexander Rosenberg. In addition to his support and encouragement, he took on the extraordinary job of editing the manuscript from its roughest form. He gave several summers to this project, and I thank him for his time, attention, and devotion.

I would like to express special gratitude to my dear friend and former student Helen Sloss Luey. In a spirit of great generosity, she undertook the job of editing the manuscript for its final delivery to my publisher. Her help enriched the manuscript immeasurably, not only because of her fine editing but also because she was able to raise questions that helped to refine my own thinking and recollecting. I am grateful to her for her labor of love.

I would like to express my deep appreciation to the Judges' Committee of the General Federation of Labor in Israel—the Histadrut—which, on July 9, 1991, chose to award me the prestigious Egit grant for Holocaust and Jewish resistance literature.

This book began to take shape in my mind over forty years ago and has been through many stages and two languages. I have shared parts of the manuscript at different times with friends and interested readers. My son Mark was especially enthusiastic throughout these years. Among the friends who read the manuscript and supported its publication was Peter Nabokov, whose ideas, suggestions, and questions were a great help. His enthusiasm gave me the courage to show it to others.

One of the readers I entrusted my early writing to was Steven Weinstock, Executive Producer at WNET Channel 13. His enthusiasm was heartwarming. I cannot thank him enough for his support and his active help in writing letters of recommendation to prospective publishers.

Johanna Plaut, a former student and friend for many years, and her husband Tom showed such interest in the story that they helped me stick with the project. I thank them heartily. Thanks also to my dear friends Sheila and Louis Menashe, Joel Agee, and Elsa Leichter. They spent many hours discussing my feelings, war incidents, and recollections. My friend Lily Bernstein reviewed some chapters with me and offered a great deal of help. I am also grateful to my friend Lodzia (Rose) Klepfisz for her generous help with the index. Victor Perrera also read the manuscript at an early stage and made helpful suggestions.

I am greatly indebted to Alan Adelson, Executive Director of the Jewish Heritage Writing Project. He read my manuscript twice, first when I submitted it to the Writing Project and again two years later when he was chosen to review it for the University of Illinois Press. Many thanks also to his editorial assistant, Isaac Mozeson, who was most encouraging. It was he who sent me the newspaper clipping about the Egit Foundation competition and encouraged me to submit my manuscript.

Other than my own family, the person who lived most closely with my manuscript for the past year and a half is my editor, Judith McCulloh of the University of Illinois Press. I would like to express my sincerest thanks to her for the faith she has shown in my project from the beginning, for the many hours she has spent editing, and for her penetrating and most helpful suggestions and questions.

I am thankful also to Anne Lewis, my secretary at the Columbia University School of Social Work, for the time and effort she has generously given to the project.

Finally, I would like to thank my dear friend Maria Rosenbloom, who not only lived through the war with me but who also gave me her active help in rereading many chapters of the manuscript. Her recollections of events aided and enriched my own understanding of situations in which we both participated. I am grateful for her friendship and unwavering support throughout the years.

Preface

How did these memoirs begin? What forces turned me toward the painful process of remembering? Turmoil and confusion were still part of me in the first years after my arrival in America, my newly adopted country. My mother tongue, Polish, was still the one I thought in while learning English. My feet began walking the new soil as I was adapting and trying to find new roots, but my heart still belonged to the continent where my youth had been spent. I was very lonely in those early days and years in the New World. I was tormented by dreadful memories of the war and living with guilt for my accidental survival.

At that time, 1950 to 1952, I lived in rural West Virginia, where my husband had obtained work in a psychiatric hospital. The little town of Spencer was, to me, a godforsaken hole where I could not find one soul to call a friend. True, I had a new life, a husband, and two wonderful little twin boys who roamed the wide outdoors—all of which should have given me happiness and peace. Why, then, was I so unhappy, so full of pain, so low in spirit and in hope? Deep down I knew what was happening. I knew that until I could give myself permission to mourn the past I would never be able to resume living. I would continue to walk with skeletons through nights of terror. I would be doomed to relive the past over and over again. I kept telling myself that I had paid dearly for my survival and ought to enjoy life once again. But my pervasive feeling was guilt, guilt for the crime of having survived while all of the others, all those close and dear ones, went up in smoke or died a terrible death from starvation and torture. These thoughts did not leave me for one moment.

One day, I took up a pencil and paper and began to scribble thoughts and memories of my war experiences. Soon I found myself needing more and more paper as I filled up the pages. I wrote without thinking. I was possessed with the urgency of getting it all down. I reached to the very core of my inner being and did not spare myself the pain of remembering. For a very long time I did not reread my notes, but went on writing. Gradually I realized that my pain was easing. My guilt began to lessen.

Sitting on the porch of our little cottage, which overlooked the state psychiatric hospital building on the opposite side of the road, my heart and mind was in the ghetto fighting for my life. At times, I had no awareness of my immediate reality. Just like the troubled psychiatric patients who lived in a world of their own torments, I still walked in the alleys of my ghetto, staring into the faces of living corpses. They, the psychiatric invalids, and I seemed doomed to live with our skeletons and our fears. I, however, was luckier than they. I had a pencil and paper and an ability to write. So I wrote, and remembered. I wrote as if my life depended on it, which in a way it did. The parting words of my dear brother Romek were with me all those days: "Blanca, try to survive to tell our story to the world." His plea now kept me going. Only when my little four-year-old sons came running into the cottage did I tear myself away from "my world." Often my children were bewildered to see tears rolling down my cheeks and wanted to know why Mommy was crying. I hugged them closely but could not explain to them that I was not yet finished with another life, one that belonged to another child and to all of our dead relatives. I resolved that one day they should know it all. Meanwhile, in spite of their being so young, I kept telling them bedtime stories—in my still-broken English—of family myths. Thus, I populated their little nursery with close relatives—a grandma, a grandpa, uncles—all people they would never know. My little sons took to those family fables and often asked me to tell them "how it was." Every story had this theme as a beginning. I was so grateful to them for wanting to know, even though they could not yet understand.

Thirty years and more have passed since the days and nights of my early scribblings. During those years I was able to return to life. What has become of me in these postwar years in my new homeland is another story.

For many years, my two sons, familiar with bits and pieces of my past, urged me to dust off my memoirs and translate them into English. I kept promising to do so when I had more time. We finally settled on a timetable. I would start after I retired from my teaching career. I did retire in 1983 and turned then to fulfill my promise. I am happy to have been able to pay this debt to Mark and Alex and to all the dear ones who were lost.

TO TELL AT LAST

Prologue

Although this story begins when the war caught up with me in 1941, its roots go back to the beginning of my life and even beyond.

I was born in Poland shortly before World War I in the small town of Gorlice and then raised in Nowy Sącz. I, Blanca Nebenzahl, was the first child, not only for my young parents, Eli and Elenore, but also for my maternal grandparents. As the only grandchild, I was pampered and adored. I can still picture my grandparents' white house on Garbarska Street, with its big backyard, its vegetable garden, and the Ropa River flowing close by. I will always remember this home as the nest into which I was born and where I spent many happy years. It was there that I felt most loved and learned to trust the world around me.

When beautiful, bouncy Romek was born six years later, my life changed. It seemed to me that this male child replaced me in the affection of those who mattered most, and I resented that. The arrival of twin brothers, Bernie and Izak, some years later did not have the same effect. By then I was twelve years old and far too absorbed with myself to bother with newcomers. The twins were just ten years old when I left home to get married, and I hardly knew them. But I was very fond of Romek, although I had some mixed emotions. He could outshine me with his brilliance, and his very goodness made me feel guilty for my own anger and competitiveness.

My grandparents, David and Rachel Ehrenreich, were pious and highly respected citizens. My grandmother was a formidable matriarch with a strong character and domineering personality. Every Shabbat evening, the whole family gathered around her table. This was a time for bringing to Grandma Rachel all the stories of the week—the "naches" (joys), the troubles, the complaints. We all shared everything with Grandma Rachel, and we received advice, praise, or reprimands as the circumstances warranted. She was the queen of the clan, respected and feared. The memories of Shabbat are still with me. I can smell the food and feel the warmth around me.

My grandfather was much softer and less demanding. He was a self-made man, and proud of it, though he often recalled his humble beginnings. He had started to work at the age of six, doing little chores for a few pennies. Through his own effort and wit, he built up a prosperous business. During my youth, he owned a tannery and also a comfortable home as well as a few other houses in town. Grandpa was an appealing character with a great sense of humor; he was much loved and respected. Although full of stories about his earlier struggles, he was never bitter.

Many years after the war, I learned how Grandpa's sense of humor helped him during the Nazi occupation. Since he was an Orthodox Jew, he wore a grey beard and short sidelocks. One day, walking toward the synagogue as usual, he saw a young Gestapo man coming toward him. It was the fancy then for members of the "master race" to amuse themselves by catching Jews and cutting off their beards. Grandfather was stopped by a rough summons from the German. "Come here, you Jewish swine." Grandpa responded to the order, holding his beard high and body upright without obvious fear. The Nazi pulled out a knife, grabbed Grandpa's head, and cut off his beard and sidelocks. Turning to the passing audience, he commented: "Doesn't that Jew look much younger and more beautiful now?" Unperturbed, grandfather reached into his pocket and asked in perfect German: "Wieviel bin ich Ihnen schuldig?"—"How much do I owe you?" The young Nazi stood there dumbfounded and finally blurted out: "Oh, this service I give gratis." In such times, it was a wonder that Grandpa got away without a beating, or worse. Truly, Grandfather was worthy of his family name—Ehrenreich—which means "rich in honor, dignity, integrity."

My grandparents had three children. My mother, Elenore, was the eldest. She had two younger brothers, both of whom had received a formal education, while mother, at seventeen, was provided with a dowry suitable to her parents' financial and social standing and "married off." The husband her parents chose for her was a good-looking, decent, smart but poor young businessman. The dowry was an effort to give him the start he needed. I remember my mother's lifelong lamentation that she was "just pushed out of my home," while her brothers received higher education. She felt very bitter about this deprivation and fought with her parents for the rest of her life for a financial payoff. She pushed us all, but especially me, to get an education. She wanted me to have the very best. The constant struggles between my mother and grandmother over money became the nemesis of my life. My mother used me as a go-between. Knowing how much my grandparents loved me, she thought my pleas would be heard. Then later she would tell me: "You better study as much as you can because your education will be your only dowry."

As I grew up, I struggled to please my parents, particularly my mother. My father seemed more reasonable and less conflicted. He tried hard to succeed in his business, but failed repeatedly. Economic depression and my mother's taste for extravagant living added to his burdens. A quiet man, he was not cut out to withstand all of the stresses of rising anti-Semitism and its effects on business. A "Christian awakening" had begun to turn shoppers away from Jewish merchants. Slogans read: "Go to your own." My father was badly hurt by this, as his best customers had been peasants who were readily influenced by the "new Christian ethic," the teachings about Jews as "Christ killers."

With all this, I had trouble studying and doing my best. The only Gymnasium for girls was a private school, which only well-to-do girls could afford. There were only a few Jewish girls there when I entered at the age of eleven. At first my parents were able, with some difficulty, to pay my tuition, but then months came when they could not give me the forty zlotys I needed. I dreaded going to school. I still recall how Professor Gottman would storm into my class and, with unconcealed enjoyment, tell me to leave the class and not return without the money. "Out with you," he would scream, adding that my absence would not be excused. I would run home in tears and beg for money so I could return to school. My father would comfort me and then plead with my mother to accept the fact that they couldn't afford to send me to school. Mother would shout that my education would stop only over her dead body. I sided with my father, as I hated to see him suffer on my account. The only solution was for me to earn my tuition money myself. When I was fourteen, I started to tutor younger children for ten to twenty zlotys per month. Within two years, I earned the whole amount. Despite increasing anti-Semitism, encouraged by the professors, I graduated with honors.

My next ambition was to study medicine. My friends and family tried to convince me that, as a Jewish girl, I would never be admitted. Because I was so naive and enthusiastic, I thought I could overcome all the quotas set by Polish universities. I applied for the entry examination at the University of Warsaw. I chose to forget that the few places open to Jews went not to those who passed the exam but to those with large bribes or political influence. When my name did not appear on the list of accepted students, I was crestfallen. I knew that Jagiellonian University in Krakow admitted Jews into its departments of law and philosophy. I decided to study law. I could work and study while living with my parents and travel to Krakow every now and then for exams. My parents thought the plan absurd and told me that my place was to marry and have children. I studied anyway.

Meanwhile, Nazi propaganda was welcomed warmly in already anti-Semitic Poland. Violence against Jewish students became a daily occurrence. There were many injuries, a few deaths. Jewish students were forced to sit alone on the left side of benches. Polish enforcers attached razor blades to the ends of canes, then burst into Jewish crowds, hitting out at random. As I was leaving a lecture hall one day, I ran into a friend from Nowy Sącz. He was Catholic, but my being Jewish had never disturbed him before. Here he tried to avoid me. I just proceeded down the stairs and was shocked to see him approach a fellow student. "Though she looks like a Slav, I know that she is Jewish. She deserves to learn her lesson. So do it!" Within minutes I was assaulted. Someone grabbed me by the hair and started to push me toward a nearby water fountain. He shoved my head under the faucet and let a stream of water run over my head and blind me. Then he pushed me down the stairs into the courtyard. Wet, bewildered, and still half blind, I stumbled while he stood over me and treated me to a few extra blows. Then another student from my hometown came to my rescue. He was a Jewish medical student in his senior year. He started to fight my attacker, but was soon thrown to the ground by a mob of Catholic students. I screamed and other Jewish students came to our rescue. Henry Mashler—soon to be Dr. Mashler—came away with a broken arm and razor blade cuts on his face. After that, I avoided Krakow as much as I could.

My parents began worrying in earnest about my marital prospects. My youthful romances were all unacceptable, as I was inclined to choose poor, intellectual, and artistic types.

Since these were hard times, my parents sublet a room in our apartment. I got to know the lodger, Max Rosenkranz, quite well. One evening he began talking about his older brother Wolf. "You two would like each other," he said. Not long afterwards, Wolf came to visit. He was a tall, lanky young man, very quiet and serious. We became interested in each other. Though I was more outgoing than he, I enjoyed his company. He was an intellectual, a socialist, and an idealist; he seemed different from the other men I knew. After he returned to Kolomyja, his hometown, he started writing to me. Wolf was good with words, and his letters inspired me with his hopes of making the world better for everyone. In person, he was reticent and did not express his feelings easily. For the next year, we engaged in regular correspondence, interspersed by rare, brief visits.

From the beginning, our respective personality needs drew us toward each other. Our relationship developed into a unique pattern of "giver" and "receiver." As the oldest of four children, I had been expected from an early age to take care of children. The "giving" suited me, and I enjoyed the role. Wolf, on the other hand, was born into his Orthodox Jewish family after seven years of waiting and praying for a child. His parents were ecstatic about him, and he was pampered. His mother died early in his youth, and Wolf grew up with his adoring father and two younger siblings. He paid for his family's affection by being "best" in his studies. In our relationship, we soon established the pattern that fit our learned roles. Even in our letters, Wolf addressed me as "Mutti" (little mother) and I used a nickname meaning "dear child." And so from early times, I became the mother he had lost, and he became the child I did not yet have.

Wolf was six years my senior and I looked up to him. I was the first girl who had interested him romantically, and this kind of relationship was new to him. I was rather shy, though anxious to be sexually awakened. Wolf introduced me to books, mainly translations from Russian classics. His letters and his way of including me in discussions of ideas made me feel wonderfully important and special. When he was admitted to the University of Warsaw to study for the state license—an exceptional honor—he asked for my hand and my help. I interrupted my studies and, for the next two years, worked to support him—first as a paralegal, then as a governess.

After we married in 1936, I joined Wolf in Warsaw. There we were drawn into a sophisticated circle of friends, including students, writers, and poets. In this group, sharing ideas with one another seemed more important than speaking of physical attraction or love. That reserve suited Wolf well. I thought that the lack of passion in my marriage would somehow change in time, and I convinced myself not to be troubled by it. And besides, I was busy with work and there was little time for "foolishness."

Wolf still dreamed of a scientific career at the university, but soon found that fierce anti-Semitism closed all doors to him. This was a great blow, as he had been drawn to science from his early years. He had had a fantasy of being admitted to the Pasteur Institute in Paris to study and work, interrupted only three times a day when someone would hand him a tray of food. This picture represented his idea of a perfect life. But since science was not possible, he decided to return to Kolomyja and start a medical practice. There, Wolf grew to be respected for his conscientiousness and kindness. I felt that I had done all I could to help him, and the time had come for me to be supported.

I soon became acquainted with Wolf's circle of friends. They too were young and idealistic, but many were less serious than Wolf. I remember the weekends and short vacations spent hiking in the Carpathian Mountains. I also remember our friends teasing Wolf for studying while the rest of us sang songs and told stories.

Life seemed peaceful until the day, about one year later, when Sam Rosenberg, one of Wolf's friends who had just returned from his studies abroad, visited us. Like others with a foreign diploma, Sam did not have permission to practice medicine in Poland. Sam was an outgoing young man, two years my senior, and I felt physically attracted to him from the start. He was the opposite of Wolf—fun-loving, romantic, a lover of music and poetry. Sam swept me off my feet. Soon after we met, we both knew we were falling in love. To Sam, I was the most beautiful woman in the world. I had never been pursued by a man in that way. I felt that the clock had been set back and that I had only then become a young girl ready for truly romantic love. For the first time, I permitted myself to question my choice of a husband. I began to think about a divorce and a new beginning with Sam. But I did not want to hurt my parents, my in-laws, or Wolf, who became withdrawn and depressed but unable to fight for or with me. There were also practical concerns. Sam could not make a living. I had just finished supporting a man for two years, and I knew and dreaded the hardships of that kind of life.

I remember the spring and summer of 1938 as a mixture of intense happiness and pain. Sam and I spent hours talking about our love and what would become of it. We became emotional and angry with each other, then forgiving, but still frustrated. We knew it could not work for us. We had to go our separate ways. Sam was heartbroken, angry, and disappointed. He left Kolomyja for Warsaw, where he began training in gynecology. I began to pick up the threads of my life with Wolf.

In 1939, the Soviet Union invaded eastern Poland. Sam returned during this period and began his medical practice, now permitted under Soviet occupation. In 1940, he married his childhood sweetheart, Gina Niederhoffer. Gina was a close friend of ours. As fate would have it, she and I gave birth to our firstborn children on the same day and in the same hospital. Our son, Zygmund, and their daughter, Anna, were born on February 19, 1941.

The first four months of Zygmund's life were wonderful times for me and my baby. We could not know then how we were about to be devoured by the monster of war.

1

How War Came to Us

World War II did not really reach eastern Poland until almost two years after its beginning in September 1939. Shortly before that, on August 23, 1939, Germany and the USSR had signed a nonaggression treaty, which included a secret clause stating that Poland would be divided between them. On September 1, Germany invaded Poland, and World War II began. On September 17, Soviet troops invaded Poland from the east. For those of us living in the part of Poland occupied by the Soviets, the war had been postponed for twenty-two months. During that time, our town and region ceased to be Poland; it became part of the Ukrainian republic, the western edge of the Soviet Union. Ethnically it was more Ukrainian and Jewish than Polish. You can still find our town, Kolomyja, on a map of Europe today. Nestled in the mountains, with the Prut River meandering by, it was then a city of fifty thousand—about fifteen thousand Jews, the rest Ukrainians with a sprinkling of Poles. We—my husband, Wolf, my baby boy, Zygmund, and me, Blanca—were the Rosenkranzes.

June 22, 1941, was a warm and sunny day in Kolomyja. I remember pushing my baby along in a stroller after an afternoon in the park, talking with several other young mothers about our children's achievements of the day. We passed a group of young people, laughing and teasing each other as they made their way to the banks of the nearby river for a swim. My best friend, Gina, pushed her stroller beside mine. The carriages glided along slowly as we lingered over the peacefulness of the scene.

"Gina, sometimes I think it's sinful for us to be living at peace here, while the rest of Europe is busy killing."

Gina looked at me thoughtfully. "Bite your tongue, for God's sake. Yes, I think about it all the time. My heart skips a beat when I think about what's going on everywhere else." She stopped and we walked on a few feet. We looked down at our children, both just four months old. I tried to smile at my little Zygmund, but my eyes filled with tears. Gina was weeping too. "What a time we picked to have children!"

We wiped our tears and parted. "See you tomorrow."

"Don't worry, we'll manage."

I had gone only a few meters further when the air raid sirens emitted their high-pitched shriek. My step quickened. As I entered our apartment building, I heard people exchanging bits of news. "The Germans have attacked." "Yes. It's a real air raid." The words paralyzed me. I was unable to move forward or back until Zygmund's cry broke my stupor. I grabbed him from the carriage and ran up the stairs.

I found my husband and several friends huddled in our flat. Their discussion was both morbid and heated; plans, advice, warnings, and interruptions all broke in upon one another. I stood there as the words slowly sank in. At the sound of *war,* I rushed to my child and held him close, trying to protect him from the very word.

The arguments continued and more friends came in, with fresh news. "The air raid was just another warning. The Germans have attacked, but there's no reason to panic. Soviet forces are going to meet the Germans at the frontier. They won't let them get this far."

Still another friend entered. "One of our people just got a mobilization notice." It was a doctor we all knew.

Wolf looked up with interest. "Is that so? Maybe they'll call me up too." His voice was full of undisguised hope.

I couldn't bear it. "What are you saying, Wolf? What will happen to me and the baby if you join up?" My shriek roused Zygmund, who started bawling. I couldn't concentrate on anything. My hands were trembling, my head splitting, nothing made sense. I lost the thread of the talk around the room. All I could think was "Why now? Why war?" It was all wrong. Why had I picked this time of my life to settle down, leave school, and start a family?

My brother Romek came into the flat and looked around. He was a young man of twenty-two. "What are you going to do?" The question didn't seem to be addressed to anyone in particular.

"The men have got to get out with the Soviets," someone said. Romek sat down and joined the group. My eyes rested on him in hope of comfort.

Romek would understand what was happening. In 1939, he'd been further west, in Gorlice, our parent's home. He had managed to escape before the Nazis reabsorbed the western part of Poland, the part they had lost in 1919. Six years younger than I, Romek to me was still a child. But he was mature beyond his years, and I often turned to him for advice and help. He was my closest friend and always understood me without need for words. As I looked at him I thought of my mother's letters of concern from occupied Poland. "Look out for the child, I beg you. I am heartbroken and lonely without him."

This child of twenty-two had already been toughened by life's challenges. He had graduated from Gymnasium at seventeen and begun work as a bank teller to help support his parents and two ten-year-old brothers. Despite his work, he found time to enroll in a university law program. He was within a year of his law degree when the war broke out. The blitzkrieg overtook his own mobilization orders and by October 1939, he was across the border in the Soviet zone and at my door. Within days he'd found work and was now head bookkeeper at a local curtain factory.

As I looked from my baby to Romek, I wondered: "What will become of the child now?" But which child was I thinking of—Romek or Zygmund?

By evening, our friends had gone, and we were alone in a deadly stillness, broken only by Zygmund's occasional whimpers. By midnight, we had made no decisions, done nothing but absorb the enormity of what had happened. The quiet was broken by the doorbell.

"Probably someone who needs a doctor. I can't face anyone tonight," Wolf moaned, slumped in his chair. But the bell kept ringing.

"Maybe it's the military police," Romek said. Slowly I moved to the door. There I found Mrs. Kahn, the wife of another physician in town, in tears. She lurched into the room and clutched at my sides. Sobbing, she turned to Wolf.

"My husband has been called up, but he's having terrible heart pains. He says he's going to report anyway. Wolf, you know he's got a heart condition. And besides there's me and Jerry." The boy was seven. "You've got to give me a certificate for him. They can't take him. He's no use to them."

"Yes, yes, sure," Wolf said reassuringly. He walked over to his desk and wrote out the statement. "This should do—they won't take him when they read this." The statement proved to be Dr. Kahn's death warrant; he become a Nazi victim two weeks later.

Wolf woke early the next morning, expecting a mobilization order. As the morning wore on and no notice came, he began to despair. When Romek suggested that, as head of a local clinic, he would probably be exempted, Wolf turned to him in bitterness.

"What'll I do then? There'll be nothing for me but suicide."

By this time I had begun to think more clearly. As director of the clinic, Wolf had become a member of the local Soviet administration, a role that would mark him for quick elimination when the Germans arrived. He clearly couldn't stay; he had to retreat with the Soviet forces. I was going to have to face the war alone.

"The only thing to do is volunteer, Wolf. Why not take Kahn's place? There'll be no question about your political reliability." Romek turned to me with a look of admiration. I didn't feel particularly noble, just scared. Like a drowning man reaching for rope, Wolf grasped the thought and held it. Rather too quickly, he convinced himself that it was the only sensible thing to do. He sprang to action, picked up a few documents from his desk, and, with hardly another word, headed into the bedroom to pack.

That morning, the street below was a scene of feverish activity. From the balcony I could see a steady stream of cars and horse-drawn wagons burdened with Soviets and their meager cargo, heading east. Between the vehicles scurried pedestrians, running their final errands in preparation for flight.

I went back inside and began to pack for Romek. "Are you going to take an extra suit? How many shoes?"

My questions broke in on his own train of thought. He looked up. "Don't pack for me. I'm not leaving."

"Are you crazy? You can't stay here. The Germans will be here in a day, in hours." I looked at him in amazement.

"I'm staying," he said quietly.

"What? Is that why you got out of the occupied zone? Is that why I've kept you here, just to fall into their grip again? Even my husband is leaving. You can't sacrifice your life in his place. The child isn't yours, and I won't let you get caught just for me."

He looked tired and had no interest in argument. "I won't leave a woman and a baby in the middle of a war. And that's it." Looking back to this day in later years, I often blamed myself for failing to convince Romek to leave us.

It was still early when Wolf and I left for the mobilization office. The Soviet officer didn't seem to notice me standing beside Wolf. "Yes, what can I do for you?"

Wolf drew himself up to his full height. "I am presenting myself as a volunteer for the Soviet forces." He went on to explain his occupation and position. "And I'll be able to take the place of Dr. Kahn."

The officer looked a bit surprised. "Well, we'll take you if you want to volunteer. Here's a mobilization order. Fill it out." Wolf almost grabbed the flimsy form from his hand. "Report this afternoon at the railway station." As we turned to leave, the officer looked up. "You must be a single man, doctor." Wolf turned back, looking quizzical. "Why do you think so?"

The officer caught the expression in his face. "Well, you seem awfully eager to get away from this town. No family here, I suppose?"

Wolf glanced toward me and replied quietly: "No, this is my wife."

"No kids, then?"

"We have a baby boy," I said.

The man looked abashed and shrugged his shoulders. "Well, good luck to you, ma'am. Your husband is making a heroic contribution to the Soviet motherland."

All I could think of was my young brother, the real hero, whose heroism I wanted so much to prevent. But I said nothing, and we left. As we walked back to the apartment, I felt hurt, then angry, and finally afraid.

With only two hours till his train left for the east, Wolf and I said our good-byes quickly. "My darling, you know how much I love you. I swear, if I survive the war, I'll come back and find you. We'll be together again, I know." All I could do was nod my head. My thoughts were not with Wolf but with my child, for whom I would need all the courage and strength I could muster.

That first Monday of the war in the east was a tornado blowing through the town, carrying its people through the streets, lunatic with fear and indecision. Some were heading to the mobilization offices, searching desperately for transport to the east. Others sought another bag of flour or sugar to hoard against the occupation that was coming. Money had become almost worthless and was scattered about in huge sums for the merest trifle. The shops were quickly cleared of everything that might be bartered against an unknown future.

At the station, as we waited for Wolf's military train, I heard snatches of anxious exchanges: questions, demands for news, cries, threats, warnings, and pitiable supplications—children begging a father or an older brother not to leave or to take them along. Some people swore, others screamed, some turned away in resignation and slowly shuffled up the platform. There were other women like me, taking leave of their husbands.

The air raid sirens began to sound again, adding their hysterical yowl to the sobs and gasps on the streets. No one seemed to notice them. We could not know it then but, though no bombs fell, those sirens signaled death for many of us left alone that day on the station platform.

Wolf's train slowly pulled out. I wandered aimlessly through the streets and eventually came across a friend, Mala, the wife of another doctor who had left on the same train. We stood looking at one another.

"What are you going to do?"

"My family is packing up. We're going to get out before the Germans get here." She stopped for a moment and then continued, as if talking to herself. "I don't know how far we'll get. The roads are jammed. The Germans will probably catch up before we get very far. But what else can we do? Julius is gone."

"I think you're right. I'd do the same, but I have the baby." I reached for her hand. We kissed quickly, and she was gone. There was nothing to do but go home.

By nightfall the city seemed empty, a ghost town awaiting a storm. Romek and I sat silently in the darkening living room. There was nothing more to say. There was nothing to do but wait and choke back the fear.

Three days passed. We hardly ate and Zygmund seemed to cry only when I put him to my breast, now dry of milk. Finally, with nothing in the house to feed him, I went out to the market, leaving him with Romek. The marketplace was abandoned. I decided to go to Gina's place. Gina too was alone with a four-month-old child. Like Wolf, her husband, Sam, had been mobilized. As I walked up the stairs to her flat I could hear the baby crying. Once inside I felt overcome by the same desperation that pervaded our home.

"So, what's it like on the streets, Blanca?"

"The streets are empty, and there's no news, nothing's happened."

"That won't last," replied Gina. "The 'New Order' will be here soon enough." We fell silent. Suddenly Gina brightened. "Look, before my husband left yesterday, he dragged in a couple of sacks of flour. Take one." I smiled. At least we wouldn't go hungry before the Germans arrived. Gina's baby began to cry again, and suddenly I remembered Zygmund.

As I rushed home, I found myself on a street crowded with people. With smiling eyes, they watched a column of Ukrainian youth form up and begin to march toward the city hall. I followed and saw the Soviet flag come down and the Ukrainian one raised in its stead. The Ukrainians were taking possession of the city.

I turned and fled homeward. As I mounted the stairs I almost ran over Romek, who was rushing out in search of me. "My God, where have you been?" His voice was filled with anxiety. "Don't you know what's going on? Ukrainian gangs are out attacking Jews. They're trapping them on the streets, pulling them out of houses, rounding up groups, and herding them to the park. There's a big sign up there: 'Death to the Yids and Bolshies.'"

Quickly we grabbed Zygmund and climbed up the attic stairway to the roof, where we could watch the streets in greater safety.

Below us young thugs were assaulting passersby, grabbing them and swinging clubs wildly as they forced them down the street to the edge of the town. There was no way to tell where they were taking their victims. The shouts and screams continued for another two hours. Then all was quiet again.

As the evening wore on, the Jews who had been trapped began to filter back to town, stumbling through the streets in a daze. Romek and I descended from the roof and stopped one of them.

"What happened to you. What did they do?"

"They made us march—about two hundred of us in all—to the statue of Lenin and Stalin that the Soviets put up last year. Then they harnessed us with ropes and ordered us to pull the statues down. They beat us with ropes and whips. We couldn't budge the monuments. And they kept whipping us. People fell choking from the harnesses and the blows. Some were trampled. Finally, the statues started to shift and then come down. After that they let us go. 'Till next time,' they said."

The next day I saw Gina's brother-in-law, battered and bruised, immobile with a broken hip. He had been among those caught. As he told his story, I felt an uncontrollable rage well up. The brutality of his ordeal seemed beyond all measure. And yet, in truth, such treatment would turn out to be easily born, compared with what the "master race" had planned for us.

2

The New Order

On June 30, 1941, the Soviet army withdrew from Kolomyja, and on July 3 a unit of the Gestapo and the SS arrived. The next morning we found notices plastered on walls all over the town, proclaiming the outlines of the New Order. The wall posters shrieked their message in three languages: German, Polish, and Ukrainian.

DEATH TO THE JEWS AND BOLSHEVIKS!
1. Law and order will be strictly maintained.
2. All orders of the occupying forces must be instantly obeyed.
3. No public assemblies without the express authorization of the occupying authorities.
4. All costs of civic administration will be borne by the Jewish population.
5. Weapons are to be surrendered forthwith.
6. Jews are hereafter deprived of all legal rights and civil claims.
7. A Judenrat will be constituted and will be the sole representative of the Jewish population.

The signs ended as they began, in equally large letters, "Death to all Jews and Bolsheviks."

The day the signs went up, a Hungarian military unit rolled into the town. The command car stopped in front of the large home of a Jewish physician, Dr. Teicher. A Hungarian officer went to the door and politely requested that his unit be permitted to use one room in the house to quarter an officer. This seemed a hopeful harbinger; it was only one room, and he had asked. Soon rumors swept the town that the Germans would move on and administration would be up to their Hungarian allies. But when the Ukrainian flag was hauled down and replaced by the Swastika, we got a different message.

The Hungarians asked for billeting space in rooms here and there. But the Germans began to take whole houses, simply ordering the occupants into the streets along with the few furnishings the Germans had no use for. But the streets remained quiet, and the optimists continued to hope. By the beginning of the second week, their illusions were shattered. Jew hunting began.

The SS formed squads of Ukrainian goons, who began to roam the city, collecting Jews off the street. Then they started to enter houses and soon had some two hundred men together, whom they loaded onto trucks and drove off to Korolowka, a nearby hamlet.

The families of these victims approached Mrs. Teicher and asked her to speak with the Hungarian officer billeted in her home to see if he could intercede. And intercede he did. When his commander arrived at the village of Korolowka, he found the two hundred men, stripped naked, standing before graves they had been forced to dig for themselves. In fact they would already have been dead had the SS and the Ukrainians not been making a sport of the proceeding, taunting and toying with their victims.

After a brief exchange between the SS and the Hungarian commander, one of the German officers turned to the men standing in their graves. "All right, Jew-swine, get your clothes on and get out of here." The Jews were so thunderstruck that they were unable to move until the Hungarian officer urged them to leave.

One of those who scrambled out of the graves and scurried back to Kolomyja was Mr. Hacker, the sixty-year-old owner of our apartment building. His son had already fallen to a stray Ukrainian bullet during the evacuation. The elderly man came into the apartment building and collapsed. In bed that night, he told me of what had happened at Korolowka, about the terror and humiliation, and the sudden reprieve. But it had all been too much for him; he died of a heart attack that night. We would live to count him among the fortunate.

Every Jew in town began to hope for a Hungarian occupation. But within another few days the Hungarian unit pulled out, leaving the SS in full charge.

In accordance with regulations, a Judenrat was established, led by a Mr. Horowitz. It became the sole liaison between the Germans and the Jewish population. The first order transmitted to the community was the demand for a forty-thousand-zloty indemnity for German war costs. To insure its delivery, forty leading Jews were taken hostage. The sum was to be delivered within seven days. Cash, silver, jewels, and gold coins soon flowed into the Judenrat. The sum was quickly amassed and duly delivered. But the hostages were not released. Once in the hands of the Gestapo, it seemed, one was as good as dead.

The second order our Judenrat transmitted was the requirement that every man, woman, and child above the age of six was to wear a white arm band with a yellow Star of David on it. Third, each person was to be registered with the Judenrat and be assigned a number. Forth, sidewalks were hereafter reserved for Gentiles; Jews were to walk in the gutter. Each day brought new regulations, new deprivations.

The Judenrat was expected to provide a daily roster of able-bodied men and women for "public work," mainly at the railway yards. At first, many volunteered, hoping to buy peace for the community. But while they worked pulling up the Polish gauge railroad tracks and laying German gauge, they were set upon by Ukrainian goons, swinging truncheons. Speed was of the essence, and the work pace was forced. The new gauge was crucial for reinforcements for the Germans attacking the Soviet Union. But the young volunteers, mostly students, were not equal to the speed and precision that was demanded. Their difficulties brought laughter and blows from the Ukrainian guards.

Anyone with glasses was marked for special attention. To the Ukrainians, glasses were the mark of membership in the Bolshevik intelligentsia. One night, a friend of ours came to my door, searching for a doctor. His face was covered with blood, and there were shards of glass protruding from where his glasses had been crushed against his face.

Early on, Romek took a turn volunteering for work at the railroad tracks. He came home that night covered with human excrement. I drew a bath for him and, while he soaked, took his clothes out and burned them. When I returned he told me what had happened. "It was a long day, but I managed to stay out of harm's way. When we were finished, one of the SS sergeants ordered the Ukrainian goons to pick out a Jew and toss him into an outhouse pit—just for fun, to cool off after a day's work. So, they picked me. They laughed as I sunk in deeper and deeper. I thought they'd leave me to drown. But when I had nothing but my head above water, one of the Germans said, 'All right, let the shit-eating Jew get out.' They threw a couple of shovels across the pit and I pulled myself out."

It was not long before the source of volunteers for "public work" dried up. The young people began to hide each morning, and the Judenrat was unable to meet its daily quota. The elders sent representatives to Gestapo headquarters, asking for more humane treatment in order to secure the required forced labor. They were told that hereafter the Germans would simply round up the required workers themselves. Thereafter Ukrainian militia cruised the streets each morning, ferreting Jews out of hiding places all over town, beating them with clubs and carbines as they frog-marched their victims to work.

One morning, my door was pounded open by a German in a rage. He pointed his rifle at me. "All right, Jew-sow, where's your man?" Behind him stood a Ukrainian thug. They forced their way in. The Ukrainian made for the closets, which he began to loot. Romek was hiding in the toilet. I ran to my crib, hoping that my baby and I might die together. The German shouted something. I turned my back, hugging Zygmund. A shot rang out, and I fainted.

When I regained consciousness, Romek was cradling my head as I lay on the floor. I had been grazed by the bullet. When he heard the shot, Romek had emerged, only to find the intruders gone. In the courtyard below lay the body of a sixteen-year-old boy. Had he been the target as he fled the building or had the bullet meant for me found another victim?

A new word entered our vocabulary: *Action*. The word sounds more ruthless in German than in English. And it soon came to be the most dreaded word we knew. It meant roundup and foretold the disappearance of victims to places no one could yet imagine.

We came to give each Action a code name, later used to mark our losses. Most Actions were named for the Jewish holidays, which the Nazis eagerly celebrated with roundups. But the first one, with its chaos and random, scatter-gun effect on the community, was simply called the Wild Action.

It was still early in the occupation, and the Jewish population of Kolomyja had not yet been forced into the ghetto. We lived all over town, and it was difficult for the Germans to know which was a Jewish home. Without help, they would have been at a loss. But the local

Ukrainians came to their aid. Some of those who had worked for wealthier Jewish families were eager to aid the Germans. Even those of us not particularly well-off could expect little protection from our Ukrainian neighbors. The young Ukrainian girl who used to deliver milk to my door had always seemed friendly. We chanced to meet one morning after the occupation began. She spat upon me and swore revenge—I will never know for what offense.

Somehow, people always seemed to know when an Action was going to occur. Just before the first one, Jews hurried through the streets to seek shelter. Then the SS officers and the Ukrainian militia came through the streets, randomly breaking down doors and herding those Jews they could find into the streets. We sat silently in our apartment all that morning.

By noon the Action seemed to be over, and people began to emerge from their homes, anxious about the fate of friends and relatives. We soon learned that most of those who had been carried off were women and children. It was hard for us to understand what this meant. For us, war was still fought between men.

About 2:00 that afternoon, three trucks rolled through the streets, filled with the victims of this first Action. As the trucks passed my door, I saw the faces of a neighbor and her two children, thirteen and fourteen years old. Their wild eyes, haunted with fear, followed me. I could not even raise my hand as they passed.

When the trucks left the town, crowds began to surge before the Judenrat, demanding intervention. Even the Judenrat's families had not been spared. A delegation was selected to approach the Gestapo commandant, Leideritz. They returned with his assurance that no harm would come to those who had "left" that afternoon. They had simply been selected for farm work, and their children would be cared for in a community kindergarten.

We were actually reassured by this news; we could not yet fathom the dimensions of the monstrousness at work. But the Judenrat wanted more information. Ukrainians were hired at considerable expense to scour the countryside to locate and tell us about these "farms." They reported that our people were indeed at work in the fields and were as well as could be expected.

"They're alive!" The news spread through the community. Other Ukrainians were hired at still greater expense to carry messages from family members to the deportees. The messages these Ukrainians brought back were not recognizable to the families. Still, many continued to believe that their loved ones were at least alive. This Ukrainian trade in messages continued to be lucrative, until the second Action.

This one came to be called the Intelligentsia Action. It began when the Gestapo demanded that the Judenrat produce the names of two hundred physicians, lawyers, engineers, teachers, accountants, and other educated professionals on the roster of Jews in Kolomyja. The two hundred on this list were swiftly rounded up by Ukrainian militia. One of them was Dr. Kahn, the man who had saved himself from the Soviet mobilization when the war began by using the certificate Wolf had provided his tearful wife. All so he and his wife could be dragged from their home, leaving their seven-year-old son to walk the streets alone, without food or shelter.

Mrs. Kahn, who had seemed so helpless only a few weeks before, proved to be strong beyond any expectation. As it happened, the sole survivor of this roundup (released because he was a member of the Judenrat) was my brother-in-law. He told me that Mrs. Kahn remained proud and defiant in the prison and tried to comfort others by assuring them that their deaths would be a heroic martyrdom to stir the conscience of the world.

The woods were close enough to town so that we could hear the rifle shots as the victims met their end. This time the Nazis did not bother about appearances. There were no fairy tales about healthful farm work in the open air.

With restrictions on contact with the Gentile population, food became a serious problem in the Jewish community. As staples like flour or potatoes ran out, we had to begin running the risk of walking the streets, exposing ourselves to the random brutality of the SS and their Ukrainian goons. And if one managed to find a Gentile with food to sell, the penalty for contact could be death.

Romek's most pressing worry became the roof over our heads. Rent for our apartment was already several months in arrears. And it was due, not to the Jewish family who owned the house but to the local German administration that had expropriated it. Eviction, we knew, would be tantamount to a death sentence. Frantically we searched for funds to keep our flat.

Some friends introduced us to a German Jew, Dr. Hertzstein, a journalist who had found himself stranded in Kolomyja at the outbreak of the war. For three weeks' rent, paid in advance, we sublet a room to him.

The day he moved in, Dr. Hertzstein told us his story. In the early thirties he had been a well-known lawyer, economist, and journalist in Germany. Then, in 1935, he had been imprisoned at Dachau for sixty terrifying days. It was the first I had ever heard about what inmates of the Nazi concentration camps suffered.

When he was released, Hertzstein and his Gentile wife fled Germany for Prague. They had already managed to get their two daughters to England, where Anglican clergymen had taken the children into their homes. In Prague, Hertzstein began to make the rounds of the legations and consulates, seeking entry visas. It took years but at last, in the spring of 1939, he secured some for the United States. But before he could use them the Germans entered Prague. At his wife's suggestion, Hertzstein left Prague for Poland, hoping to make his way to America from Warsaw. But to leave Poland he needed another visa. His Polish exit visa arrived the day the Germans attacked Poland. In flight again, he found himself in Soviet occupied Kolomyja. For almost two years, Hertzstein tried to validate his exit documents and leave for the United States. But again he was overtaken by the German army, which was attacking the Soviet Union. Hertzstein had survived all this time by tutoring English.

As I listened to this odyssey and gazed at this man prematurely old and worn, I began to feel ashamed that we had demanded rent in advance. We quickly made Dr. Hertzstein feel like a part of our family. As long as he was with us, our evenings were diverted by his many stories and his varied experiences.

Just as the problems of food and rent were becoming insoluble, our fortunes turned. Romek was called back to his position in the accounting department of the curtain factory where he had worked under Soviet occupation. The Germans had converted it to uniform production and reopened it under its original Ukrainian management. The factory was directed by a woman known to us only as Lydia. She had always liked Romek and had the greatest confidence in his work. Romek was eager for the job. It offered a conduit to non-Jews who might help us with food and other needs. And Romek's job protected him from the press gangs collected in the streets daily to work on the railroad tracks.

As the Intelligentsia Action receded from immediate consciousness, people breathed a little easier. But all too soon, fear struck again. It began to be rumored that the Germans were seeking a young Jew who had served with the local Soviet militia during the Soviet occupation. Having failed or declined to flee with the occupiers, he had to pay with his life at the hands of the Ukrainian militia.

Despite a thorough search of the town, the Germans never found their target. So the Judenrat was informed that it had two hours to deliver him up to the Gestapo or another search would be launched, a bloody one.

The thought of another Action brought a throng of people to the door of the young man's eighty-year-old grandmother. The crowd begged her to reveal his whereabouts. The old lady could respond with nothing more than sorrowful pleas of ignorance and the pitiful offer to sacrifice her life in place of his.

As the crowds milled about in front of her house, news came that the Germans had already launched their own search. They had sent a militia unit, along with guard dogs, into Mokra Street, the poorest Jewish quarter of the town. As the dogs growled and snarled, men ran for cover. The few women and children found along the street were dragged to the pavement, kicked and trampled by the dog handlers rushing into hiding places. Those they found who did not immediately surrender were shot. Within an hour, the dead and dying were in the alleys up and down the street, and the SS was driving another herd of victims toward the city prison.

When the Action was over, Mokra Street was awash in blood. We never knew whether the former Soviet militiaman was ever found. No one cared. The price of his freedom had been paid by others. The forest of Szeparowce witnessed another mass execution. As the sound of the rifle shots died, this Action received its name—Mokra Street Action.

Late that night, an eighteen-year-old Jewish boy appeared at the Jewish hospital. He was trembling and incoherent. A bed was found for him. The next morning I came to the hospital to visit my father-in-law. Dr. Zeiger, chief of the small facility, invited me into his office. His face was drawn, and as we sat down, tears began to run down his cheeks.

The young boy had been among those rounded up on Mokra Street. They were taken from the prison late that night and driven in trucks to the woods. Like previous groups of prisoners, the victims were made to dig their graves by the light of lanterns the Ukrainian guards held over them. Then they were commanded to strip to the skin. One of the guards took out a harmonica and the victims were ordered to dance. When the Jews failed to obey, they were set upon with truncheons. Following this entertainment, they were sent through a close-order drill by the German officers: attention, at ease, squat down, jump, run . . .

When the fun was over, the Jews were ordered to face the trench they had dug. The firing began. As the bodies fell, some protected others from the bullets, even as the dead pushed the living down beneath them into the ditch. The boy was one of those saved by the bodies of others. Suffocating, he struggled up through the bodies above him and broke through the ground, without a thought to the guards still at the scene.

As he raised his head he could see that the Germans were gone and the Ukrainians were busying themselves going through the clothes left by their victims, drinking and arguing about the spoils. Unnoticed, the boy slipped into the woods and watched as the trench was filled and flattened. After the trucks carried the militia away, the boy made his way back to Kolomyja.

The story left me without words. The director rose and put a hand on my shoulder. "A few more Actions like this and the Germans will have a town free of Jews altogether. If only we had been more concerned with guns than food, military training instead of the Talmud, we might have died with some honor. . . . Now . . ." He stopped, his thought hanging incomplete. "Be brave. You're young and fair. Maybe you'll be spared."

We had experienced three Actions. After each, we had picked up the pieces of our lives and gone on, reassuring each other that we would survive, if only to bear witness. Mothers would meet, talk about their children, share their food and their hopes, watch the babies play, laugh, and grow—as if there were a life for them to look forward to.

3

Present and Past

By this time, Romek could hardly make himself go to work each morning and leave me and the baby defenseless in the face of another Action. It must have been a miracle that our place had been overlooked the day they rounded up the "intelligentsia." The very day Wolf left, the local Soviet radio had made special mention of his heroic departure to serve the Soviet army. Surely, some of the Ukrainians who had listened knew that he had left a family behind. Several friends urged me to leave the apartment and hide. But both Actions had passed over us, and we remained in the doctor's large apartment, with its consulting room and sign on the door below.

Romek would not allow us to press our luck further. He began to search for some place we could move outside of town. Several Jewish families had found shelter among the rural population. After some time, Romek located a farm family living several kilometers from town. They had a shed, consisting of a room and kitchen. The three of us would sleep in the room and Dr. Hertzstein in the kitchen.

The day we moved in I began to breathe a little easier, and so did Romek. Zygmund too became a little less frightened and began to play outdoors in a small garden where he could pick at the flowers and tease a puppy. Another boon was that the family owned a cow, so we could buy milk for him daily and occasionally add some chicken and eggs.

With Romek's ability to barter for food in the Aryan world and Dr. Hertzstein's meager earnings, we were able to keep our heads above water. Now and then Hertzstein returned from his private tutorials with a piece of ham or a bit of lard, given in payment by his Polish friends.

As fall approached, I began to feel that the worst might be over; perhaps we would survive after all. We began to think about keeping our little shack warm through the winter.

One day early that fall Romek came home without his white arm band and with an anxious look on his face. It could only mean new trouble in town.

"Thank God, you're all right. There's a new Action in town, the worst yet. They've set fire to the synagogue, and they're forcing Jews into the flames. They haven't missed a house on the street, as far as I could see.

"There's about a hundred Ukrainian militia, led by a couple of SS men. They broke into the factory and grabbed hundreds of Jewish workers."

I interrupted. "How did you get out?"

"Someone came into the office just before the SS got there and told me they'd seen you in the roundup with the baby in your arms. I pulled off my arm band and got here as fast as I could." He leaned down and reached for the baby playing at his feet. Hugging and kissing Zygmund he made for the door.

"Why another Action?" I asked. But he wasn't listening.

"Grab the baby, and let's get into the barn."

Why the new Action? It was simply because of Rosh Hashanah and Yom Kippur. Alone in our shed, I had simply lost track of the days. But the pious Jews of Kolomyja had not. Despite the ban on public meetings, a small group of elderly Orthodox men had quietly gathered at the house of their rabbi. Their prayers were fervent but secret. How could the Gestapo have learned of them? We concluded that the crime this gathering constituted had been discovered by Ukrainian townsfolk, who duly reported the meeting to their masters. In the midst of their prayers, the doors of the house were broken down and the old men, wrapped in their prayer shawls, were thrown into the street. They were driven by gun butts and kicks toward the synagogue, already aflame. As they were pushed to the flames, the guards hissed: "Now, pray to your God for mercy while you turn to ashes." The cries of the victims were mingled with the Shma Israel.

We learned later that several hundred Jews had eventually been killed in the blaze and in the streets. Others who were spared the flames died a more humane death—they were simply shot after being herded into the Szeparowce woods just outside of town.

For a time after the Yom Kippur Action, things seemed quiet. There were a few minor incidents: terms of imprisonment for using the sidewalk instead of the gutter or for hoarding forbidden food. But we were no longer under any illusion about the Germans' aim: to make the town Judenrein (free of Jews). But first, they had to clean out the hamlets surrounding Kolomyja, forcing the Jews who lived there into town, where they could be more easily controlled. This preoccupation gave the city a respite.

Meanwhile winter arrived. We spent the evenings huddled by the kitchen stove, sitting in the dim light of a candle, listening to the wind whistle through the loose boards of the shed. None of us had the energy for a book or a conversation. At most, we'd glance at the German propaganda sheet Romek or Dr. Hertzstein brought home. It was replete with victories and heroes. Vainly we tried to read between the lines, wondering whether anyone knew about us, whether anyone cared. Could the British or the Americans simply observe our destruction from afar? Did they even know about all of the murders? Even if Hitler were to lose the war, we would still be its innocent victims.

Dr. Hertzstein was the oldest of us, but often he seemed the strongest and the most optimistic. It was he who would break in on our somber broodings with diversions and suggestions. One night he proposed that we pass the winter nights learning English. We just looked at him. He could read the question in our eyes: Is there still a world out there where they speak English?

I often accused Dr Hertzstein of being too passive. "Why didn't you ever fight them? You're just a typical German, all you can do is follow orders."

He took my jibes in good humor. "Blanca, I'm older, I've been through Dachau." And he shrugged. What Romek and I would have given for a machine gun and the chance to scream our hatred as we defended ourselves.

After the war, I often met people, even Jews who survived the war in Siberia or elsewhere, who asked, in all innocence, why we hadn't fought back, defended ourselves, taken a German with us to our deaths. "Why," they would ask, "did millions of Polish Jews simply allow themselves to be led meekly to the slaughter?" How were we to answer this question? We described women holding babies in their arms, clutching the frail hands of children, whose men had died defending them with bare hands. Who among us would have taken the luxury of attacking a guard when the result would be not just our own death but that of a hundred more, all still clinging to life? We could not choose for others, and so we could not choose for ourselves.

The beginning of 1942 brought new rumors, all suggesting that the Germans would move the Jews of Kolomyja and its environs into a ghetto. By the end of January, Dr. Hertzstein came home with hard news. "The Judenrat has announced a new German regulation. All former citizens of the Reich deported to Poland in '39 have got to report to Gestapo headquarters for registration tomorrow."

I stared at him. "But you're not going are you? It's certain death."

"Don't worry. It'll be all right. After all, we're German nationals. They can't just liquidate us. Anyway, it's an order."

Romek joined my protest. "Get out right now. Take to the woods, hide. You'll probably be able to link up with partisans somewhere."

It was no use. The next day, Hertzstein duly went in to register as a former German citizen. He didn't last a day. He was received at headquarters, taken to the Szeparowce woods, and shot. Altogether twelve hundred Jews who had foreign passports were killed that day.

For Romek and me it was the first taste of death for a member of our "family." Hertzstein had lived with us and shared whatever he had, he'd been helpful, and very fond of Zygmund, sometimes spending hours playing with the little boy. While we were consumed with anxiety, he always seemed to have time for this small child born at the wrong time and to the wrong parents.

That night, Romek and I sat before our meager dinner, unable to eat the bread before us, thinking about the man whose chair was now empty.

"I never really could understand the man," Romek observed. "He always seemed to be more German than Jew."

I knew exactly what he meant. "Yes, he so loved the culture, the literature, the music. For him the Nazis weren't German."

"I couldn't bear to listen to him defend the German nation against us. When he got on that high horse, 'Ich bin ein Jude, wahr, aber vorallen bin ich ein Deutsche' (I am a Jew, yes, but first and foremost I am a German), I just had to turn away.

"Sometimes we'd argue. I told him that the Jews in Germany had just forgotten who they were. If Hitler had not hated them so, they would have been as loyal to the Reich as any other group.

"It must have been a harsh experience for all those German Jews,

Polish by accident or oversight, to get dumped at the frontier in '39. But even after that, they wanted nothing to do with the rest of us."

I nodded. "Even Hertzstein, in the end, remained loyal to a fiction. He was glad to die a former German citizen, along with his fellow countrymen, separate from the poor Polish Jews killed in the same woods."

Such talk did little to console us for our friend's death. Still more bereaved was Zygmund, who went about for days afterwards, searching for his friend and asking plaintively for "Der Tag," as Zygmund called him. Each morning Hertzstein used to sweep the child up in his arms and say "Guten Tag"—good day. And when he returned home at night, as often as not a small surprise would appear—a hunk of white bread, a bit of candy, or a lump of sugar.

As Zygmund looked about for Der Tag I wondered how to comfort him for this loss. If I used the word *German* to explain, he would run off to hide. To him, the word meant only that it was time to be still and take cover.

Late that night, as I tried to sleep all I could think about was who would be next. I drifted off, only to be awakened by a sharp rapping at our door. Romek lurched from his bed at the same moment. It had to be the Gestapo. I began pulling a few clothes together for Zygmund, so that he might go to his death warm.

As Romek opened the door, we saw not the Gestapo, but my cousin, Paula Bergman, standing cold and breathless at our door. Paula lived with her husband, a physician, in the town of Zablotow, hundreds of kilometers away. She was still trembling with cold as she collapsed in fatigue at the table and began to tell us what had happened.

"It was the Liquidation Action." She seemed to know we would understand her. "I managed to escape, and I've been running forever to get here. I don't know what happened to the rest of the family."

It was the end of sleep for us that night. We sat around the table till almost dawn listening to Paula's story and then to her plan. It was simple and courageous. She would remove her arm band, with its yellow Star of David, and secure a fictitious birth certificate in a Gentile name. And then, with her husband and family if she could find them, she would head for some large town in eastern Poland.

As I listened, the plan began to attract me. "Surely we could do the same," I asked Romek.

"No, we can't." He replied. "You've got a little boy who is circumcised. We'd never get away with it. Don't you see? If it weren't for him, I would never have let you stay here this long. You're blond and blue-eyed. You wouldn't have any trouble by yourself. But with him, you'd be finished if you left this place." He was right. I could only hug my baby tightly to me and sigh.

Paula stayed with us for a week. Each night was filled with long conversations. Our talk moved back and forth from our childhood and hometown to the present tragedy in which we were living. Somehow Paula seemed to me no longer to be simply my cousin but a distant heroine who had cheated death.

Mostly we talked about happy times, about our lives as young girls and women. I had always admired Paula's fascination with Zionism and Palestine, her idealism and commitment. But Paula spoke of admiring me too. We had both struggled to accomplish something in our youths.

Those evenings with Paula made me look back at so much of my life, reflecting on events that had been almost obliterated from my memory by the months since June 1941. What had it all amounted to, all the hopes and plans, the sacrifice and self-denial? Hiding in a shack with my baby and my brother. Would it simply end here?

I resolved that I wouldn't let that happen. I was going to fight to the bitter end, for Romek's sake, and for Zygmund's.

After a week, Paula left. She was going back to Zablotow to find out if her family and her husband had survived.

CHAPTER

4

Ghetto 1

As spring approached, the lengthening days and warming sun lulled us into a complacent optimism. But on the very first day of this 1942 spring, the spell was broken by a new regulation, shouted out in German Gothic and Polish from posters all over town.

As of March 21, all Jews were to relocate themselves to one of the three officially established ghettos in the town. There was to be one in the area between Kopernik and Wałowa streets, a second around Mokra Street, and the third on Dzieduszycki Street. Each was to be fenced off from the surrounding area, leaving one point of entry and exit. Order would be maintained by a Jewish police force, supervised by the Judenrat. People were permitted to carry into the ghetto only what they could hold in their arms. No vehicles could be used or operated inside.

I stood amidst a group of Jews, reading the fine print of the regulations posted on the outside of the Judenrat, listening to the curses and laments, the sighs of despair. The meaning of these new regulations had not fully sunk in as I headed back to our shack on the outskirts of town. As I walked along, careful to avoid the now-forbidden sidewalk, I saw ahead of me a small group of old friends, Lonek and Celia Rothenberg. They were carrying something. As I tried to catch up, I realized it was a casket. But they were moving quickly and unobtrusively through the streets, avoiding the glances of passersby. Despite the briskness, it was indeed a funeral procession. When I finally caught up, Celia did not stop, but explained: "It's mother. She died last night, and we've got to bury her while we still have a chance."

I had known Celia's mother. "I'm so sorry . . ."

Celia nodded. "At least she died in her bed, surrounded by her children. And she'll be buried in a marked grave in a Jewish cemetery."

Celia was right. Her mother was one of the lucky ones. It was the last Jewish funeral I was to witness for three and a half years.

The next day was marked by frenetic activity as thousands of Jews rushed into the empty ghettos, searching for a place to claim as their own. All three districts were in the poorest Jewish quarters; their buildings were cramped and old. To come within the space allotted to each person and to accommodate the newcomers, old occupants had to pack their families into an even smaller living space than before.

The streets were bedlam—women laden with clothes and with small children in tow; men carrying firewood or food, a table or a chair. One man staggered groaning under the weight of a couch strapped to his back. The fortunate ones were pushing prams and baby carriages piled high with their possessions. Somehow the Germans had forgotten to prohibit pushcarts.

The day was a perfect evocation of the Jew as eternal wanderer. Each person struggled under whatever could be carried or moved, knowing that sometime soon a shirt to barter would be the difference between hunger and starvation.

As night came, the relocation seemed to be complete. The Jews of Kolomyja settled in and fell asleep where they could.

Before the war, we had known some people who had a house on Kopernik Street. They had been permitted to stay on, in just one room. With their help, Romek got us one of their newly vacant rooms. We thought ourselves lucky. Kopernik Street was the best of the ghettos. We did not realize how fortunate our choice had been. The house on Kopernik Street backed onto the ghetto fence, a fact that saved our lives more than once.

We were allotted space for four, so Romek, Zygmund, and I added a new member to our family, a young lawyer I had known at home in Gorlice. Herman Kramer had clerked with me for a local lawyer before I moved to Warsaw with Wolf. Like Romek, he had fled the German occupation in '39. So the four of us settled into a room of pitiful dimensions, furnished with nothing more than a sofa. Later, as the ghetto grew more crowded, we would grow to a "family" of eight.

We sat there on the sofa, surveying our worldly goods. Each of us had carried what we could into the ghetto. Zygmund had managed to bring his teddy bear and a little stuffed dog. He could not know that

his treasures were ours as well; Romek had sown a few rings, brace-
lets, and wristwatches into them—all we had to barter against the
harder times to come.

Between us, Romek and I managed to salvage from the apartment
a small loveseat, two chairs, and a cabinet. As more and more people
moved into our room, even this furniture had to go. In the end, only
Zygmund had a mattress; the rest of us slept side by side on the floor.

From the moment the ghetto gates were locked, one thought alone
began to obsess us all: getting out. Jews with jobs received a "work
card," which entitled them to leave the ghetto for work in the Gentile
sectors. Working Jews—for the roads, the factories, and for the railway tracks—were essential to the German war effort. Those who
worked were called the war-priority element of the Jewish population.
Though they worked from sunrise to nightfall without rest or food and
under constant threat of random beatings, these Jews were the fortunate ones. Just getting out of the ghetto was recompense enough for
their labor.

Romek worked in a garment factory, officially as a bookkeeper and
unofficially as the assistant manager. A hundred other Jews worked
there as well, as tailors or boot makers, producing uniforms for the
Wehrmacht.

Only young men qualified for a work card. The old, women with
children, and the ill had no chance to secure one. Those who hoped to
use their work card to improve their lives or that of their families ran
great risks. Though a worker might come and go, no one could bring
food, fuel, or anything else of value into the ghetto. Each person was
provided a half a kilo of bread each week. Workers were searched by
the Jewish police and the Ukrainian militia each night as they returned
from work. Anyone caught trying to supplement the ration from outside the ghetto was shot.

Members of the Jewish Auxiliary Police—the Judische Ordnungs-
dienst—seemed to take a special pleasure in their grisly duties. At first,
responsible members of the Jewish community came forward to serve
in the Judenrat and the Jewish police. They did their best to represent
Jewish interests and to soften the force of German regulations. But
when they realized that their work, especially with the Jewish police,
amounted to collaboration, these men gave up their jobs, leaving no
one but bullies and beasts, eager to outdo their masters in cruelty and
abuse.

Locked behind the ghetto walls, we met each new day with increased apprehension about the next Action. The far-sighted began to prepare elaborate hiding places, to which they could retreat and survive a new attack unnoticed. We had become particularly apprehensive about Jewish holidays. These seemed to be occasions for specially gruesome roundups. The first holiday to be observed in the ghetto that year was Passover. Like the year before, Jews could sense the attack to come. Rumors circulated wildly, men and women began to check their hideouts, keeping their ears cocked for any special activity or disturbance in the streets. On Passover eve, a dense silence fell over the ghetto. Scraps of information from the Judenrat, an overheard Gestapo conversation, passed from person to person. Then a neighbor came by. "It's coming. Tomorrow. I have a friend in the police. He moved his family out of the ghetto last night . . . so brace yourselves . . ."

What could we do? We couldn't run. Where could we hide? Fear swept people from the crowded ghetto streets as the Ukrainian militia came up to the gate.

Sometime before, we had excavated a sort of a hole in the basement to hide in. But as I grabbed Zygmund, I realized that the others already in it wouldn't welcome a mother and her crying child. There was nothing to do but stay in the room and wait to be caught and rounded up or just to be shot where I stood, holding my baby. At least Romek and Herman would make it, I consoled myself. They were outside the ghetto, working in the factory.

Zygmund looked up at me. "Why are you crying Mommy? Have I been a bad boy?"

"No, darling. It's the Germans; they're the ones making me sad."

Suddenly the door began to shudder from the force of blows. But when it opened, instead of the Gestapo or a Ukrainian guard, there was Romek.

"Give me the baby. Let's go." Romek led me down the stairs and out to the street, heading for the ghetto gates. When we got there the Ukrainian guard snarled us away. "Get back. No one out. Orders."

Back at our door, I turned on Romek. "You were safe at the factory. Now we'll all die together. You fool."

Without replying Romek tore off his Star of David arm band and then reached for mine.

"What do you think you're doing?" But I knew. The thought of escape paralyzed me.

But Romek was already heading for the fence behind our house. I followed, with Zygmund in my arms. There were no guards on either side. Romek took the baby and helped me over. Handing me Zygmund, he climbed over as well.

We found ourselves on a deserted street outside the ghetto. There on the other side stood the home of Lydia, the manager of Romek's factory. We walked across and up the steps. After a knock, the door was opened by Lydia's mother.

"Please come in," she smiled, looking down at my frightened little boy. "Why don't you use the bathroom. Wash up and refresh yourselves."

Later that day, Lydia's mother took all three of us to the factory. It was strange being out without my arm band, using the "Aryan" sidewalk, trembling about an action I would not have even thought about before. As we walked along, the older woman repeatedly tried to calm me. "Don't rush along, relax. Pay no attention to passersby. Just act like you're my guests. I'm showing you the town."

I did not begin to breathe easily until we got to the factory. As we stood in the director's office, overlooking the shop floor, I looked out the window, from which I could see a small part of the ghetto. I was sure I could hear shots and the piercing screams of women and children. Turning back to the factory floor below, I saw the Jewish workmen glued to their benches. They knew what was happening. Each of them had families beyond the ghetto wall. Their looks of desperation were unbearable. Some had lost control and began weeping.

All I could do was find a niche behind a mountain of cloth and sewing material. I sat down and held my frightened baby in my lap. While I tried to calm him, my thoughts were with friends and their children, still in the ghetto.

Zygmund and I sat in that corner well past nightfall. There was little movement elsewhere in the factory. Most of the men seemed to have turned to stone. Occasionally, one would pass me on the way to the sink for a drink of water. Close to me I could hear a woman moan. She had left three children in the ghetto. Later, another woman fell down in a faint. Those around her rushed over to revive her. As she came to, all she would say, over and over, was "It's my fault, my guilt . . ."

As the afternoon turned to dusk, we began to hear voices growing louder. Soon it became apparent that they were German soldiers, shouting and cursing. We rushed to the windows. The gathering darkness was pierced by the glare of streetlights. And beneath them we could see a forlorn column of Jews from the ghetto, hundreds of families, being herded along by guards.

Like others, I strained to recognize a face in the file. I could hear others gasp as they spotted a friend or a child, a mother or an uncle. Those "fortunate" enough to find a face in the night beyond the factory windows soon began to break down. As they fled the windows, cursing their fate as survivors, others took their places. Like people lining up, those who eventually got to the window gave their places to others and threw themselves to the floor, rending clothes and wailing in their impotence. To us inside, the people outside were already dead . . . we were merely seeing their ghosts.

I put Zygmund down in a corner and returned to one of the windows. I was transfixed by the sight of those hundreds of victims, some crying, some impassive, as they were driven along like cattle. I winced at the blows I could see falling on laggards. Yet as I searched their faces, I could see no individual I knew. Every face looked the same; all wore the expression of death.

As I watched, an old woman staggered and fell to the ground. An SS officer approached, looked down at the body beneath him, took out his luger, and carefully fired into her head. I could not hear the shot, but I could see the body jerk and become still. . . . Others in the herd could do nothing but walk past the bleeding corpse.

Suddenly, from what seemed like a long way off, I heard Romek's voice. "Thank God we saved you. It looks like they've rounded up a couple of thousand. They must have killed hundreds in the ghetto." The numbers meant nothing to me. I had become numb.

By early evening, the streets were empty again. The workers were beginning to move around, wondering what the morning would bring. Some pulled on their coats and headed back to the ghetto, hoping against hope to find families they had hidden in bunkers and cellars. Those who had found their families through the window the night before remained. Mainly, they sat still on the floor, sitting shiva (mourning).

The factory cleaners had come in to get the shop floor ready for another day of work, a day no different to them from the last. The rest of the workers got up to leave, knowing full well that they would be back the next morning to work, to survive another day.

As Romek and I made ready to go, Lydia approached us. "Blanca,

Romek. There's no reason to go. Spend the night here. I think there's going to be more trouble. If you go back they won't let Blanca and Zygmund leave when they open up for the work detail in the morning."

We agreed. Lydia led us to a small apartment occupied by the night watchman, an elderly Jew and his family. He greeted us warmly.

"My wife and daughters are getting ready for the Seder. Won't you join us?"

As I looked across to the dining area, I realized it was the first night of Passover. I could see a white tablecloth and a pair of tarnished silver candlesticks. Our host handed us each a Haggada and led the way to the table.

As the old gentleman led us through the traditional service, my mind wandered back to Seders at home, their family joy and warmth. Then I looked down on my son, settled on my lap, joining in the singing and the smiles.

When our host passed around the bitter herbs, to remind us of rigors of slavery in Egypt, I had to leave the table. It was too much. How could their bitterness compare to ours? I recalled how we children were excused the bitter herbs at my family's Seders. We were secure in the knowledge that mother and father would never let a shadow fall upon their children. And today I sat at the Passover table with strangers, after a massacre of so many children. What protection, what joy could I offer my child? I knew he would never live to ask the four questions at his father's Seder table.

A. This picture of me at age fifteen was sent to a friend in Gorlice. She survived the war, hiding in France, and returned the picture when I visited her in Paris in 1960. B. My gymnasium picture.

Maria (*left*) and I in Warsaw, shortly before my departure to Germany in 1944.

These ghetto pictures were taken by the Nazis for identification purposes. Duplicates of these were rescued from the Gorlice city hall files after the war by Jewish survivors and reproduced in a memorial book. These copies came to me through my family in Israel, who got them from the memorial book. A. My father, Eli, at about fifty-two years of age. B. My mother, Elenore, at about forty-eight. C. My brother Izak at about seventeen. D. My brother Bernie at about seventeen.

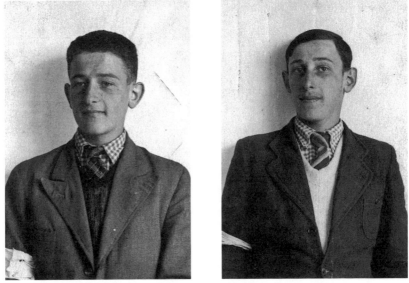

Joseph Korzenik, my cousin, the first relative discovered after the war. The photo was taken about a year after his liberation from a concentration camp in West Germany on April 23, 1945.

This photo of Menek Goldstein was taken in Kolomyja in 1945, one year after his liberation.

Sam Rosenberg as a major in the Soviet medical corps, 1941.

Nunek Najder, Maria's husband, who was killed in Kolomyja when he was twenty-five. This picture was given to Maria by her brother-in-law Celek when she visited him in Poland in 1991.

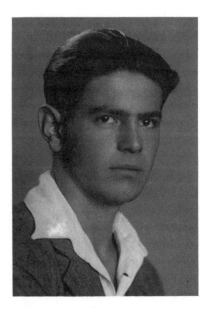

Zygmund Rosenkranz (*top*),
December 1941, ten months old, and
with Romek (*bottom*) in one of the
last pre-ghetto photos taken in 1941.
These two photographs survived the
war because they were sewn into the
lining of my coat.

Frania with son Leszek
(Alex) in Lwów in 1943
when they were both on
false identity.

Maria Rosenbloom (Mati)
in her UNRAA uniform in
Germany, 1946.

GRIECH.-KATH. PFARRAMT

in ~~ГР. КАТ. ПАРОХІАЛЬНИЙ УРЯД УСПЕНІЯ ПР. Д. М.~~

Kreis *Lemberg*

Distrikt Galizien.

№ 2047

Bescheinigung

Es wird hiemit bescheinigt, dass ~~Herr~~ /Frau *Bronislawa*

Panasiak Tochter des Demeter geboren am *4. XII. 1915*
und Anna geb. Boczkowska

in *Lemberg*

~~Ukrainer~~ /-in und Arier /-in ist.

Diese Bescheinigung ist für die Arbeitsämter, Polizei und Zivilbehörden im Reich ausgestellt.

Lemberg den *9. October* 1942

Печатка і підпис

Julian Pyorowytch
Pfarrvicar

This birth certificate—used as a racial identification document—was given to me by Lydia. She got it from her brother, a priest. It was the real birth certificate of a Polish woman, Bronislava Panasiak, who had died in Siberia. Note that she was identified as "Arierin"—an Aryan.

This identity card, or Kennkarte, was issued to me by the German occupying government in Poland on January 30, 1943, and was good for five years. I obtained this document through regular channels using my new birth certificate. It made me legitimate as a Pole of the Greek Catholic religion.

CHAPTER

5

Ghetto 2

After a sleepless night sitting around the table watching the candles burn out, morning came and the first workers arrived. There was no need to ask them questions. All our answers were written indelibly across their faces. They picked up their needles, scissors, and yardsticks and set to work.

Almost everyone had lost family. The streets of the ghetto were filled with corpses. No one had removed them. There was no place to bury them. Those who had survived in hiding remained there. No one could say whether the Action was over or not. As Passover still had a week to run, we guessed that our tormentors were not through celebrating.

Indeed they were not. As the workers left and the ghetto gates closed that morning, a cordon of Ukrainian militia began to surround the walls. No one was going to jump to safety. The last to leave for work could see squads of SS entering the ghetto, this time with dogs lurching forward with noses to the ground, sniffing for human flesh. Soon, no doubt, all the hiding places would be uncovered.

In the factory, we could not know what was happening. Little work was done, and as the gloom of nightfall gathered, no one so much as moved to turn on a light.

But then, beyond the windows, someone noticed a brightness. Again, we rushed to the windows of the shop floor. It was a fire, consuming the entire Kopernik ghetto. As we stood in unbelieving terror, a door was flung open and in rushed a youth. Several workers turned to question him. Before they could ask him anything he began.

"I managed to get out. The Germans are burning the whole place down." He was sobbing. "When they began to discover the hiding places, they were furious. So, they decided to just roast the people who were hiding. Anyone who came out was shot by the Ukrainian guards. They shot them as they leapt from windows or came up out of cellars."

As he continued, he became even more distressed. "Women were throwing their children out of the windows of the burning buildings. Those wood frame houses ignited like dry tinder. Then the wind just carried the flames from one place to another . . . Must be a thousand people burned alive in there."

As the boy finished his story, the phone rang in the director's office. Lydia went over to it. Romek moved to her side. After a moment she covered the receiver. "The SS is heading here."

Romek turned and came toward me and Zygmund. He grabbed me by the arm and swept the child up. "Come on," he ordered, and made for Lydia's office. Lydia followed. Once the door was closed behind us, he glanced imploringly at her and then pushed Zygmund and me into a closet. In the darkness I could hear the lock close.

After what seemed like only a minute or two, I began to hear the sound of boots in the office. Then German voices began.

"I want a list of your Jews essential for war work."

Lydia replied: "I need all the ones I've got."

"Forget it. You've got eight hundred. Cut it in half."

"I tell you they're all essential to meet the production quotas."

At that point I could hear the SS men turn and leave, slamming the office door behind them.

They had moved down to the shop floor and were making the selection themselves. As they walked among the benches they picked the older people, pushed them away from their work, and pointed them to the waiting Ukrainian guards.

Dimly I could hear a woman's voice. "Please, I left two babies in the ghetto. Can't I just see them once more . . ." Suddenly there was a shot—and no more pleas. Half an hour later, three hundred Jews had been driven out of the building by whips and clubs.

When they had gone, Romek came over and unlocked the closet door. Zygmund had fainted from lack of air, a blessing that saved his life. The slightest whimper would have called attention to us.

As I came down to the shop floor again, I heard little besides expressions of resignation and hopelessness. "What's the use, even a work pass is no protection. I'd just as soon die now as later."

That evening we made our way back to what was left of our ghetto. As we entered, we saw the survivors, listlessly emerging from their hiding places. They began to ask about family and friends, and soon we could hear the moans and wails as they learned what had happened.

Up the stairs in our room there was nothing but broken furniture and torn bedding. The Ukrainians had worked the room over, searching for Jewish gold. Failing to find it, they had broken the one or two dishes lying in the sink and the windowpanes. For good measure, they had also tossed the bits of stored food out into the gutter below. Looking out the window, I could see people bent down at the curb, scavenging what could be saved from the filth. Near them I saw a pair of people going through the pockets of a corpse as it lay in the gutter. Nearby, a body stirred, still alive, probably calling for water or help. He was ignored by the living, too busy searching for children or parents who just might have survived. I began to detect the odor of death wafting up from the ghetto streets.

This second Passover Action reduced the ghettos to two. Those who had lived in the one burned down and who had survived began to filter into ours, seeking shelter. Before they had even found a roof for the night, the sound of guns could be heard again. People began to run for cover once more.

Romek had gone back to the factory. Zygmund and I were alone, cowering in our bare room, awaiting our own final end. As we crouched against the wall listening, the shooting grew distant. I lay Zygmund down on a scrap of mattress to sleep and ventured down the stairs into the street.

There I saw people scrambling out of their hiding places. "What happened?" I asked.

"Looks like they're heading for the other ghetto," someone replied. "Maybe we're safe for the moment."

When the survivors finally came to our ghetto we heard a now-familiar story. The Ukrainian guards came through the streets, shooting those who had not hidden and pulling those who hid out into the streets and shooting them. Those undiscovered died in the fires. We had heard the shrieks as the buildings came down.

By 5:00 that evening, there was smoldering silence where the ghetto had been. Outside our ghetto gates we could see the Gestapo leading their Ukrainian militia smartly away from the charred streets.

A little life came to our ghetto that evening with the return of the factory workers. As they came through the gates, I rushed to search for Romek. I found him and led him to our room, where he slumped down on the floor. In the dark he looked decades older than his twenty-two years. Vainly he tried to cuddle Zygmund. Above the smile, I could see the glistening tears. His face turned to a grimace despite his efforts.

Now that Romek was home to watch the baby, I was able to go around to the second ghetto to see if any friends had survived this latest Action. There were several others with the same idea, and the Ukrainian guards let us pass through the gates with only a laugh and a curse. A few minutes later, we were walking through the charred remains of Bóżnica Street, a street we used to know well as Synagogue Street. There were smoldering ashes where neat frame houses had been. Walking was slow, for we had to take care stepping over bodies. As I picked my way around them I felt my legs begin to give way. I tripped and fell over the still-warm body of a young woman. I shrieked and rose quickly to my feet.

A few feet further on I could see a small group of children, between two and five years old, surrounding the body that must have been their mother. They pulled at her and spoke to her, not understanding death. All they could see was that their mother lay before them uncaring. Their kisses had turned to pleas. "Mommy, wake up, why don't you answer." One of the children bent over and hugged the corpse. The horror overwhelmed me and I ran blindly from the spot, thinking only of Zygmund enacting the same scene.

I found my way to the street where Celia and Lonek Rothenberg lived. It was Celia's mother who had thankfully died in bed the day before the ghetto notices went up.

Approaching their house, I found a group of people in heated argument. One man insisted: "Just let him bleed. The sooner he's dead, the better for him and for them."

I interrupted. "What's it about?"

The speaker turned to me. "It's a question of whether you try to keep alive someone who wants to die. We've got a guy here who's slit his wrists after he found his family dead."

It developed that he had kept his wife and children hidden through several Actions in a shelter he had constructed. But that morning, he had come back to find them dead. "Can't tell how they died. But he just sat down and took a razor blade to his wrists."

I looked at the group in amazement. "Why are you debating about it. You've got to save him."

The reply came from several voices. "Why? For what? Save him to use up an SS bullet? A couple of minutes more and he'll find peace."

I was insistent. "Show me where he is. Maybe I can do something for him."

"You a doctor or something?"

"No."

"Then leave it alone. . . . We're all under a death sentence here anyway. It's just a matter of time."

Feeling a mixture of disgust and hopelessness, I walked away. Miraculously, I found my friends still alive. "Thank God you're still OK," I said as I entered their room.

"Yes, but for how long?" It was Lonek, as despairing as the others. Hopeless, he too had given up the struggle for survival.

The mixture of helplessness and hopelessness was too much for me. I embraced my friends and returned to my ghetto. Passing the offices of the Judenrat, I learned that fifteen thousand lives had been lost in this Action.

The ghetto had been officially reduced to two districts. Food became the most pressing need. Every able-bodied adult sought work outside the ghetto walls. Even mothers of young children tried to get permits to leave the ghetto. Working on the outside had become the only way to smuggle food in. Without it, the old and the very young began dying of hunger.

Once the food was gone and the water cut off, the old and the weak began to come out into the streets of the ghetto begging for a crust or something to drink. From the window of my room, I could see the human skeletons staggering through the streets, while emaciated young mothers sat at the curb, offering dried breasts to children who did not even whimper, but died quietly in their mothers' arms.

Sanitation broke down and disease began to sweep the population. I grew weak and no longer left the room. Listlessly, Zygmund and I passed each day waiting for Romek and Herman to come home. Each night as they returned from the factory I looked to their hands, not their faces, in hope of food or drink. And almost every day there would be something. A bit of bread, some flour, something from their Aryan co-workers.

Romek never seemed to want any of the food. I knew he was going hungry for Zygmund and me. Often after a day at the factory, he would jump over the ghetto wall behind our house and prowl the Gentile districts for hours, stopping at farms of Poles we knew before the war, begging, bartering for milk. Romek had designed a rubber pouch that he would strap around his waist, which the guards who did the body searches at the gates never noticed.

Others without such stealth were not so fortunate. The guards were Jews themselves, and it was not easy to fool them, for they knew the ways to survive as well as we did. Often they would discover smuggled food, and in their anger simply toss it to the dirt and grind it under their heels, watching milk meant for babies soak into the ground. As it trickled away, the old and the infirm gathered at the ghetto gate might be allowed to fall to their knees and literally lap it off the ground before it disappeared. Sometimes not even this was allowed. At other times there were too many at the gates to stop, and then the guard would simply turn with a grunt and retreat to his post.

How could they justify such cruelty? "Look," they would say, "I have a job to do. If I don't do it, it's my life at stake and my family's."

At this point, Romek managed to get some Gentile friends, like Lydia at the factory, to write to our parents in Gorlice. Until then, messages to the German Reich, where Gorlice now lay, had been by the briefest of cryptic messages on postcard forms supplied and censored by the Gestapo. A code had sprung up to circumvent the censorship. A card that complained that uncle "Busar" or aunt "Lechem" were dead meant that meat and bread were no longer to be had, for that is what these words meant in Hebrew. When a card said that "malach amuves" (Hebrew for *angel of death*) had visited the family, its recipient would understand.

All that Romek and I knew about our parents was that they were still alive. Now, by sending letters through our Gentile friends and theirs, we were able to have some news of my parents' conditions in the Reich. We were relieved to learn that there was as yet no ghetto in Gorlice. The German Gauleiter seemed humane and even permitted Jews to earn a feeble living trading with Poles for food.

We decided that we had to tell our parents of our starvation. As a result, food packages soon began to arrive for us at the homes of our Gentile friends. They were small boxes—three loaves of bread, a bit of sugar, and some flour—crucial to those weakening in the famine. But Romek's problem was how to smuggle them into the ghetto.

Each week when a package arrived, he would arrange to meet Lydia in the night at a spot along the ghetto wall. She passed the parcel over. Each night this happened, I waited in dread for Romek to return. Were he caught it would be death for him, and for Lydia as well. As the eternity passed, I sometimes heard a shot ring out from one corner of the ghetto or another, as a Jew was caught trying to escape. Each time I was certain it was Romek, buying bread with his life.

Lydia's bravery saved us just as it saved the Jews of her factory, where far more were "employed" than production warranted. But she did much more for us out of her admiration and affection for Romek.

As our situation receded from the brink of death by starvation, our family increased again. One evening Romek came home with a young Jewish boy from, of all places, Vienna. His family had been stranded in Kolomyja by the start of the war, and his parents had died in the recent Passover Action.

The boy was close to total emotional collapse. He had remained inside the factory for months, neither moving from his corner of the building nor even eating enough to stay alive. He would talk to no one. Romek befriended him and brought him out of his shell and into our small room. Romek and the other two men slept on the floor, while Zygmund and I shared the remains of a broken-down lounge chair, the only piece of furniture left.

The week our new lodger came, new disasters struck. All the neighboring towns and villages in the region were finally to be declared "Judenrein"—free of Jews. Those Jews who had survived the years of Nazi occupation in the region's hamlets were ordered into our horribly overcrowded ghetto. Thousands were driven into the streets, already cramped with dead and dying. They came with nothing on their backs or in their hands, for they had been forbidden to carry anything whatever with them from their homes. After miles of forced marching, they arrived before the offices of the Judenrat, begging for food and water.

There was nothing to do but lodge them in the already overcrowded tenements that lined the only street of the ghetto. These new inmates searched for relations who might take them in. Among them we found the father-in-law of my cousin Paula, who had spent the week with us two winters before. The rest of the family had long ago left their small town, Zablotow, and made for Tarnov, which, like other towns in the west of Poland, had been absorbed into Germany. But the father declined to go. He looked too Jewish and would jeopardize the entire family. So he had stayed behind and found himself with us. So there were six in our garret.

Each morning, the four men would leave for work, or for the streets, while I remained behind with Zygmund. I sat for hours surveying the littered streets. Below, the scarecrows shuffled along with bellies distended from malnutrition. For days at a time, I would not venture out and remained motionless, conserving my strength to live another day, but thinking all the while, "And what if Hitler loses? Can a people so devastated be reborn? No. He will lose. But when civilization returns, it will be too late for the Jews."

In the latest Action, the Germans had rounded up six thousand people, loaded them into cattle cars, and transported them to the concentration camp at Belzec. How they died we could not be certain, but rumors were circulating that they were gassed. Others said they had been driven into minefields and torn to pieces. All we could know for certain was that the Szeparowce woods no longer rang out with a fusillade of shots immediately after each Action. That meant the Nazis had found a more efficient way of killing.

But just leaving us to languish in the ghetto seemed a costless means of killing us. Our dwellings had become living cemeteries—their occupants still breathed, but they were no longer among the living. Death beckoned us in the stench that rose up from the bodies rotting in the gutters where they had died days before. Every few days an emaciated horse would draw a cart through the streets. The bodies would be heaved up on the cart and permission sought to bury them in a ghetto ditch. We came to call the cart and its horse the "Messiah." We could only envy the dead for having been delivered from this world by this rickety old wagon pulled by this tired old horse.

We became experts in malnutrition, our own and that of others. First the flesh began to hang off the bones, revealing their shapes and sizes. Then the feet and legs began to swell. After that the stomach started to protrude until people began to look like balloons with appendages. By then they could no longer stand or walk very far. They just lay down in the gutter and waited for death. As they waited, some summoned the energy to raise their hands and beg a crumb of bread from a passerby. But soon we saw nothing except a lifeless shape that used to be a man, a woman, or a child. The only thing to do was cover the face with a scrap of litter.

6

Crushing the Ghetto

On lucky days, the men returned from the factory with a bit of food, and I made "dinner." More often than not, all they would bring was a bit of grain. I ground it carefully in an old coffee mill I had somehow preserved and moistened it with a bit of water drawn from the muddy liquid that came out of a nearby street pump. The meal would be portioned out, and we would all gulp down our share before a neighbor could come by and beg a mouthful to keep her child alive. But we never denied a person in need. To be sure that at least Zygmund would get some miserable portion every day, we pried up a floorboard so that each morning we could hide for him what little we could spare.

Along with the constant hunger came typhoid, which killed its victims painfully but quickly. There were still some physicians in the ghetto, but they had no medicines. Once the only hospital in the ghetto had been abandoned for lack of funds and supplies, many doctors simply gave up any attempt at succor.

Yet not even typhoid was a certain killer. My friend Gina contracted it and lay for weeks in a camp cot with a high fever, without food or fluids, next to her fifteen-month-old baby—yet she did not die. She didn't even infect her baby or the other woman and child living with her.

Several weeks without an Action tormented us with apprehension. But suddenly one morning, the Nazis appeared in the ghetto's streets and began shooting. Caught unawares, many people were in the streets and could not reach their hiding places. Our house was among the furthest from the gates, so we had time to take shelter in a dark space we had built under the stairwell. But by the time I got to it, there were seventy people in the hideout. They were not pleased to see another person, and with a small child at that. I could feel the daggers as they surrounded me and Zygmund. I began praying. "Please God, don't let the child cry out." One sob and I would murder seventy souls. Some around me whispered the words I was thinking. I clutched Zygmund to me and whispered endearments. "You must be quiet, dear. The Germans might come and get us."

"The Germans, Mommy?" As the words emerged, I could feel the child tense up into tears. And then we could hear the shouts of the soldiers above us as the trapdoor groaned with their weight. I could hear the door to my room break, and then the sound of shots mingled with screams and snarling commands in German.

The tension was too much for Zygmund, and he burst into shrieks. Before I could do anything, two large male hands wrapped themselves around his throat. And even before I could begin to scream, the same hands reached for my throat. I fainted.

When I came to, I was in my room, lying on my broken-down lounge chair, with Zygmund playing at my feet. A neighbor woman was with me.

"We were sure lucky you and the child blacked out," she said. "Saved the lives of all of us in that hole. Once the Germans left, the guy who knocked you out brought you up here . . . They rounded up another two thousand for the cattle train to Belzec."

That night Romek returned from work in the sure conviction that he would never see us alive again. His mournful face turned to joy as he opened the door. Crying like a baby, he hugged us both to him.

But from that day on, Romek was no longer content that we simply rot away in the ghetto. My parents had written through the Gentile connections that we should smuggle Zygmund to them in Gorlice. They still had an income and there was as yet no ghetto. So each night, Romek raised the question. And each night my refusal provoked a quarrel.

"All they want is for their only grandson to survive. They'll even send a courier to bring him through to the west . . ."

"No. I won't be parted from him."

Romek would quote my mother's letters to me. "It's utter selfishness," he would tell me, "to think so narrowly. You're not going to prove you're a fit mother by protecting your baby personally until they kill us all. Your mother is willing to find a Christian family to take him so he'll survive, no matter what happens to us or them."

For all their logic, these arguments had no effect. I couldn't bring myself to think of parting from my child. Even the knowledge of what other mothers had been through with children they would not part from did not move me. Some had been forced to abandon babies in their cribs; others saw their children suffocate in airless hiding places. We had all seen the Germans catch a child on the street and use the toddler for target practice. A friend had even throttled her own son to protect the hiding place of a hundred others. The luckiest children I knew had died by the cyanide their mothers had saved the instant they had been discovered. Still, I was going to keep Zygmund, no matter what.

But the near escape made Romek implacable, and he decided to take the matter out of my hands. Secretly he wrote to our parents, telling them that our only chance at survival required them to take the child. One night, after we'd eaten our gruel, he looked at me seriously and spoke.

"A woman has come from Gorlice, a Gentile. She's at Lydia's. She's here to take Zygmund back." My jaw dropped. But he continued. "We'll pass him over the wall behind the house tonight."

I shrieked: "You can't. He's mine."

Romek glowered. "Do you realize what this has already cost your parents, you selfish little child?"

"I don't care." I reached out and grabbed Zygmund to me.

The woman returned to Gorlice without my son.

A week later, there was a quiet knock on our door. We opened it to find one of the elders, a member of the Judenrat. He was a distant relative, and he had come to deliver a notice.

"The Gestapo has ordered the Judenrat to hand over several hundred children tomorrow, for transport." I gasped. "Look, if you panic, Blanca, and word gets out, I'll be killed.

"I heard from your father-in-law that you have a chance to save your boy's life." He stopped for a moment. I said nothing. "I lost two children in the Dzika Street Action."

"Yes, I know . . ." My voice trailed off.

"I'm here because my telling you may save one Jewish life." With that, he turned and left.

The Germans had made my choice. And there was little time to lose. We could not know how soon the children would be rounded up. Romek rose, put on his threadbare coat. "I'm going to jump the wall.

I'll go to Lydia's and wire Gorlice. Maybe we can get that woman back before it's too late."

The next night Romek came home with news. "She's here already, and we can give Zygmund to her tonight."

"I won't give him up, not unless I can see the woman first." So, that night I went over the wall behind our house, Romek handed Zygmund to me, and he followed. Cautiously we made our way to the old secondary school that used to serve the neighborhood. There at its gates I met the righteous Christian who could carry my child to safety.

As I handed my baby over I could not hold back the tears. I felt my entire past life collapsing behind me. I felt I would never see the child again. Blindly, I followed Romek back to the ghetto wall.

By the time we had returned to the room, the tears had ceased. All I could feel was a deadness. I sat down in the chair, not responding to anything that was said to comfort me. After a brief attempt, the three men withdrew, and by their own silence showed how much they recognized and respected my grief.

The next morning the Children's Action began. By judicious bribery, the Judenrat was able to mitigate the effect, but still many children were taken.

Zygmund's departure heralded a new period for me. The morning after I handed him over, Romek woke me and bodily forced me out the door, down the stairs, and out into the street. I was to go with him to the factory. Once there, I was given a place at a workbench along which women, young and old, bent over old silk stockings, carefully unraveling them for the thread. The thread was to be used for parachutes. So our work was war priority.

With both of us at work outside the ghetto, our material situation improved. We could trade with Gentiles for food and consume the food my parents sent without the risk of having to smuggle it in.

More significant to me than the food were the letters from my parents, reporting on their grandson. He was thriving and giving a great deal of joy to them and the rest of the family, including my younger twin brothers. It made me happy, yet apprehensive. Nothing more was said about placing Zygmund with a Christian family.

With the conviction that Zygmund was safe and a bit more food, my spirits and appearance revived. I could share the letters and pictures of Zygmund with my friends, content at least in the happiness he was providing his grandmother. But when I met less-fortunate women, friends and strangers with emaciated children hugged to their breasts, my spirits sank. Had I betrayed them by saving my own son from the fate that awaited their children?

"No," these friends replied. They were happy for me. Knowing that just one child was safe strengthened them in their struggle to survive. I helped them when I could, sharing what food I could get into the ghetto.

At this point, the Judenrat was forced to set up a soup kitchen, where a watery soup was provided each day. And despite the many Actions, the numbers in the ghetto increased from week to week, as Jews from outlying hamlets were driven into it. So each day, more and more people crowded around the kitchen, and not even the rumor of an Action was enough to drive them away from it. The queue for soup began early in the morning, long before the kitchen was open. There was much shoving and pushing in the line, and at its head one could hear the word *thick* said insistently, imploringly, as the hungry would demand a piece of cabbage leaf, a vegetable, or a root in their portion of warmed water. Those too sick to line up had to make do with a weekly ration of bread.

The factory remained a haven for those who could still work. Each morning, a few hundred of us could leave the ghetto for our war-priority work. As a newcomer to Kolomyja, I had not known many of my co-workers before the war. But our common fate and shared goal of survival drew us together. Many of the women who worked with me did so only to bring food to their hungry families in the ghetto. At work, their ears were always tuned to rumors of action or unrest. At the first hint of trouble, they would fly back to comfort and protect their children, not thinking of themselves.

Each day it became harder and harder to smuggle food into the ghetto. The beatings increased and became more severe. But it remained a bit easier for women, who were not so intimately searched as they passed through the gates.

The old and the sick were no longer in the streets. Only the young and strong had a right to survive. The Jewish Auxiliary Police searched from house to house, clearing cellars, garrets, and hiding places for those who could be handed over to fill the Judenrat's quota. The SS's demand for bodies seemed insatiable. And the Jewish police knew that any shortfall would have to be made up from their own families.

People would do anything to protect themselves from deportation.

Orthodox Jews shaved off their beards and sidelocks in an effort to look young and strong. Women unable to obtain work cards bought forgeries that might protect them in an Action. Underground work took on a feverish pace, as bunkers and hiding places went up to replace those that were discovered. Activity was fueled by rumors that the Germans were having setbacks on the eastern front. We knew that even "tactical withdrawals" and "shortening of the front" would lead to fearful liquidations.

As I worked in the factory one June morning, we noticed four SS officers enter the ghetto. Anxiety filled the shop floor. Another Action? No. Four officers without Ukrainian militia could only mean a new demand on the Judenrat, not a full-scale attack.

But it soon became clear that this was indeed a new Action, one in which the members of the Jewish police were made to be the shock troops. We saw teams of them herding groups of the elderly and infirm, along with children, toward our factory. Before reaching it, the victims were forced into the old Jewish ritual slaughterhouse, which stood across from the factory. We heard the moans and the shrieks as the militia's blows hurried the stragglers into the building. Those who fell were shot by the SS or bludgeoned to death by our own Jewish militia.

Horror within us was swept away by shame for our own Jewish police, some made wretched by their own actions, others seeming to relish it. Lydia came over to the window to watch.

"Beasts," she said. I turned to her and she continued: "It's unbelievable. Don't those young men know what they are doing? Driving their own people to the slaughterhouse? Do they think their lives will be saved by complicity? They'll die no differently from those they send out on today's transport . . ."

I had no answer. So I kept looking steadily out the window, tears streaming from my eyes. I tried to take in every detail. Inside, there was the staccato of machine-gun fire. I could see some old people attempting to escape through a window being dragged back in. At the entry stood the four SS officers, smiling, smoking, passing the time, as the Jewish police brought more and more victims from the ghetto to the slaughterhouse.

Looking to the ghetto gates I saw that Jews no longer ran or resisted, but just walked unescorted up the street to the site of execution—

resigned, surrendering themselves, unwilling to struggle any more to preserve life under such conditions. Only the young still put up any resistance, kicking and biting at the Jewish police dragging them from hiding places.

Suddenly, movement on the roof of the slaughterhouse caught my eye. It was a young boy, perhaps seven or eight. He had come out of a chimney and crouched at the pinnacle of the pitched roof. Slowly and cautiously he began making his way down to the base of the roof on the side facing the Gentile quarter of town. My eyes followed each step as I prayed for his safety. I glanced down at the SS men immediately below him, who were too busy enjoying the depredations around them to look up. The tension within me was unbearable. And then it was broken. I saw that a Jewish police officer had spotted the child and called out to one of the Germans. The Nazi nodded, drew his luger, and unhurriedly took aim. The boy fell dead at his feet. The SS officer put his pistol away without taking any further notice of the boy's body.

I turned back to look at the street. There through my tears I could see an elderly couple slowly making their way toward the slaughterhouse. As they came closer I recognized my father-in-law and his wife, Wolf's stepmother. Silently I took my leave and expressed my love for them.

In the last few months I had shared my food with them. I had kept my father-in-law out of the hospital when he was sick, so that he would not be taken from there for transport. He had made me promise that should Wolf and I survive the war, we would light Shabbat candles every week. He knew we were unbelievers, but he accepted my promise to fulfill his last wish. This very morning, like all others, he had gone to the synagogue to pray for the health and safety of my child, his grandson, and for his own strength and wisdom. Now he was about to be executed in a place where cattle were slaughtered.

At the end of yet another Action, again I thought to myself, "I can't take any more." My nerves were shattered beyond recovery. My heart was numbed with pain. I had seen too much, and the price I was paying for my own survival from one day to the next was just too high.

The roundup of the old and the very young at last brought quiet to the streets of the ghetto. No longer were the weak and the lame begging and dying in its streets. The young and strong still in the ghetto began to talk about escape. Stories circulated about those who had gone to the Gentile section, living on false identity papers or without any cover at all. Those who were caught paid no higher price than we could expect to pay if we remained.

Romek and I began to consider the possibilities. He was all for it—for me that is.

"You can do it, Blanca. Not me. With my looks, I'll never get away with it. And if they catch us together, nothing will save you. I'm going to die anyway. I'd rather it be here, among my own people."

I listened carefully. Even for a woman like me, with blue eyes, blond hair, Germanic looks, and unaccented Polish, the risks were very great. Romek was probably right about his own chances. Mine were not really much better.

Besides, our every move was carefully monitored. In fact it was only a few days later that we learned of the arrest of a young physician in the ghetto, Dr. Marmorosz, and his friend, Lieberman, a pharmacist. They had been planning an escape to the Gentile side and had given money for fictitious Aryan documents to a Polish middleman—who promptly reported them to the Gestapo and received a bounty for his efforts. Dr. Marmorosz was the luckier of the two. He managed to hang himself in his prison cell. Lieberman was taken out to the cemetery, forced to dig his own grave, and shot.

Others who managed to leave the ghetto tried to make a run for the border, hoping to get to Hungary or Romania. They disguised themselves and often tried to travel by rail with non-Jewish friends or paid Gentile companions. When caught, they were shot on the spot or sometimes returned to the ghetto to be hanged in the public square as a warning to others.

A couple I knew, a dentist and his wife, made it as far as the railway station platform, where a former patient recognized them and eagerly pointed them out to the Gestapo. They were taken off the train, along with the Gentile friend who had secured the tickets and was traveling with them. The Aryan suffered his friends' fate. It was no surprise that even one's closest friends were unwilling to help.

At the factory, production began to slow down. Supplies and raw material were becoming harder to get. Workers began to take greater pains with each piece, knowing that as soon as the material ran out, their status as war-priority workers would end, and with it their lives.

Lydia conspired with this slowdown. Only when a German visitor toured the factory did the work rate pick up. At other times there were opportunities to talk and exchange experiences, to draw strength from each other, and to share sorrows. I began to have a special fondness for a girl several years younger than me named Mati. I could not know that we were destined to share many experiences in the years to come.

One afternoon, I noticed Mati surreptitiously reading at her workbench. I took the book from her and looked at the title. To my surprise it was *Pan Tadeusz*, a great classic of Polish literature by Mickiewicz.

"You're sitting here reading a classic? How can you even think about it?" I inched closer to her, in admiration. She was a kindred spirit.

Mati looked at me. "I can't help it. I studied literature at the University in Lwów before the war." Soon, we were trading passages recalled by heart from our favorite Polish poets.

From the moment my friendship with Mati began, there was a purpose in my day. Getting to the factory and my workbench acquired a meaning. It seemed to give Mati a new lease on life as well. We would often talk of the past, the countryside we used to tramp, the peaks of Czarnohora we had climbed, walks along the Prut, the warm sun and friendships of the world before the war.

Mati was married to a pharmacist. Remarkably, her entire family was still intact, parents, sisters, nephews. It made it easier for me to tell her about Zygmund, to show her the snapshots and share my hopes for my son. Like everyone, she admired Romek and recognized my good fortune in having such a brother.

Until August 1942, when Zygmund had been gone for six months, the leniency of the German authorities in the west seemed to continue. Messages came almost daily, keeping us informed. Then suddenly messages ceased. As two days stretched to a week without news, my heart began to sink. Romek tried to calm me, but I was prepared for the worst. After two weeks without word from Gorlice, my Gentile friends began to express annoyance with my inquiries.

"Anything today?" I would ask.

"No."

"Are you sure?"

"Yes."

"Can you check again?"

"I told you. If I get anything, you'll be sure to know. Leave it alone."

At the end of three weeks, there came a letter from one of my younger brothers, Bernie. The news was terrible.

One day without warning, the most thorough Action possible swept through Gorlice, a total liquidation. As it began, those few who had prepared bunkers and other hideouts took shelter. My parents had built a particularly good one, and they had managed to climb down before the Germans arrived. But Zygmund gave them away! He had begun to cry and could not be controlled. The SS were attracted by the noise and soon found the entire family. Like the rest, they were marched to a local shoe factory, where a "selection" was in progress. Left—death, right—work. The family made its way through the lines, my mother comforting her grandchild. My father understood that their destination would be the east and extermination. As they came to the head of the line, they could hear the German call for volunteers to go to the labor camps. My father made his twin sons step forward. After much resistance they finally did. At seventeen, they were healthy and strong. They easily passed screening for the labor pool on the right side. The rest of the family was driven to the railway station and shipped to what they were told was an "unknown destination" in the east.

Two days later, the boys were sent to a work camp at Krakow-Płaszów. The letter my Gentile friends had received was addressed from there. Naively believing the Germans, they beseeched me to find out what I could about these farms in the east to which my parents had been sent. They were rumored to be in the vicinity of Belzec. Perhaps, the letter suggested, I could send word there. "It's so much closer and maybe you have a chance to save the baby." Their hopefulness made me want to howl. In Kolomyja, there were no illusions about Belzec.

Romek and I looked at the postmark of the letter: August 17. So, this was the day we had become orphans. I could only hope that my son had died in his grandmother's arms before they reached the gas chamber.

Romek and I sat in silence for some time. He had been particularly close to our father, and soon he broke down completely. The tormented energy inside me needed release, and I found myself on my knees scrubbing the wooden floors of our little room. I felt I would go insane with rage and grief. As the energy flowed out, I was able to collapse and let go.

As darkness fell, we sat unmoved. I couldn't help thinking I had killed my son by delivering him, and my parents too. Now I wanted to die as well. But with morning came the desire to get out and seek the distraction and security of the factory.

The size of the ghetto had grown to ten thousand, as more Jews were herded in. The streets were filled with beggars in rags. Orphaned children wandered aimlessly around the corpses, slaking their thirst at the gutter. No one prevented them, no one could even respond to their piteous pleas. The only able-bodied men on the street were the members of the Jewish police, who strutted by swinging their truncheons. Their reward for serving the Reich was an extra ration, big enough to leave some for sale to those with money left. Those few could no longer afford the luxury of sharing. Everyone had become an island. There was no compassion, no attempt at self-respect. Sharing a morsel of bread with another became a supreme sacrifice. The alleys were full of wretched skeletons struggling to find a rind or a leaf in a trash heap. A rusty can of stagnant water was all a dying mother would beg from her children.

We could not even comprehend that beyond the ghetto walls a world existed in which people led ordinary lives. We would walk to the factory in disbelief as we saw people normally clothed and shod, healthy and dignified. And they would return our looks of incredulity with disgust. Like lepers, we were shunned and feared. Even those moved to pass a bit of bread to one of us were careful not to make contact, fearing the diseases of the ghetto.

By the end of August, news of new German victories replaced the previous announcements about tactical withdrawals. We greeted the news bitterly. Nevertheless, some among us remained convinced that the Germans could not win. But we could hardly expect to survive to the day of their final defeat, not, at any rate, in a ghetto in occupied Poland. Some took the war into their own hands, choosing death by spitting at a German or resisting a drunken Ukrainian rapist. But our admiration for such heroes was tempered by the cost their heroism inflicted on us all in reprisals, hostages, and increased deprivation.

Sometimes we thought about the partisans, who had taken to the forests to harry German supply lines and shoot stragglers. We gave but little thought to the masses of Soviet armies arrayed against Hitler, nor could we know that much of our suffering was communicated to them by the Soviet government, to spur their efforts. Indeed, some among us disbelieved what we heard of the statistics, thinking them Soviet propaganda. And if our own people living the hell could not bring themselves to credit the enormity of the the genocide, how could we expect America or Britain to do so?

In early September, the ghetto seemed unconsciously to brace itself for a new Action. When we learned that the head of the Judenrat, Horowitz, had committed suicide, panic set in. If so privileged and well-informed a man saw no hope, we concluded that there was none to see. People sold anything they had to buy a work permit and secure the status of war-priority labor. Anyone with the badge of war-priority labor was the envy of the rest of the ghetto. The unemployed would besiege the Judenrat daily, imploring the counselors for such status. Instead, with each passing day the Judenrat presented the Gestapo with a new list for deportation. With Horowitz's death, the council had lost all semblance of a role as protector of the Jewish community. Meeting in secret, they closed their ears to the hapless crowds that surged at the doors of the Judenrat.

The storm broke on September 15. That day and those that followed remain with me more sharply than all other memories of the war.

I was working in Lydia's office outside the ghetto. Early that morning a message was delivered from the German command, requiring a complete list of those absolutely essential to the operation of the factory. This list, plus all the people not on it, were to be delivered to the Gestapo. This list could contain no more than two hundred names. The other eight hundred laborers were to be dispatched for transportation east.

At the end of the day Lydia called Romek into the office.

She handed him the order. "Romek, you've got to make the list. I will not do it."

He began to speak but she interrupted him. "No, I can't make this choice for your people . . ."

Romek replied: "And you think I can? These are my blood. You can't make me master of life and death for them." He handed the order to her and left.

That night we sat in the darkness of our room, then shared with five other people our age, each immersed in private thoughts and premonitions. We knew there would be another Action, and that this time it would sweep the factory workers along with those already doomed.

Suddenly the silence was rent by the clatter of shoes on the stairs and then a rapping on our door. In some fear we said: "Come in."

A crowd of men, women, and children burst in, stood over us, and shouted at Romek. Through the cacophony, we soon learned that news of the list had leaked from the Germans into the ghetto, and rumor had it that Romek had agreed to make it for Lydia. And then the crowd fell on us, offering money, jewelry, silver, along with demands, entreaties, prayers, that one or another be included on the list. Romek rose and tried to calm them. "No, you're wrong. I have not agreed to make any list. I won't have anything to do with such a thing."

No one believed him. The crowd grew and stretched down the stairs and into the street where it numbered in the hundreds. No one would believe that this slim twenty-three-year-old boy would be unwilling to take such power. Even as they collected their bribes from the floor and retreated, they did not believe that Romek was telling the truth.

The next morning a new edict was plastered up on the walls of the Judenrat. All inhabitants of the ghetto were to present themselves for registration the next day. Workers were to form into a special group. We were all to march to a soccer field behind the Labor Exchange offices. The leader of each factory team was to have a list of workers to present to the Gestapo. The notice ended with the usual demand for order and obedience, along with the penalties for failure to comply.

Members of the Judenrat tried to reassure the crowds. "This means there'll be no Action, no killings, no deportations. It's not a trick. They just want an orderly registration of the inhabitants. They gave their word! But dress in your best, appear neat and presentable."

A few in the crowd accepted this announcement with relief, only because they wanted to believe it was true.

At the factory that morning, Lydia was surrounded by her Gentile foremen, composing the required list. It took much of the afternoon, and when it was finished she presented it to Romek. His name was at the top, under the designation "master tailor." Feverishly he searched it for my name and found it among the "seamstresses." After a few minutes of silence, he handed the list back to Lydia. "I can't remain on this list under false pretense, and I won't live if it means at the cost of someone else. I'm no tailor. Put me down as what I am, a bookkeeper."

"But that's not a war-priority position. You won't have a chance."

Romek was adamant. "Change it or remove me from the list."

Lydia relented, and Romek mumbled thanks to her for placing me on the list. "Hers is the only life I want to save."

I stood in the corner of the office listening to this dialogue, mute with fear for myself and my brother. Then Lydia went down to the shop floor and dismissed the workers for the balance of the day. She urged them to do what they could to save themselves. Most remained, milling around the factory, knowing full well what the registration really meant.

What was I to do—register or hide? I really didn't want to live any longer. I almost longed for the release of death. It was my brother who had to survive. He had to live . . . I repeated it to myself over and over as I walked back to the ghetto. As we walked, strangers approached, asking me and others the fateful question, "Register or hide? What do you think?"

My instincts answered: "Hide. It's a trick." But as for me, I had decided to go to the roundup point, because I knew Romek would be going. When my friends asked why, I shrugged. "What's left? My baby's dead, my parents and brothers too." I parted from my friends at the ghetto gate.

CHAPTER

7

The Ghetto—End and Escape

I stared at the bushes and twisted underbrush. I thought I would head back to my room but found myself instead drawn to the little stream, Młynówka, a filthy bit of water that meandered down the edge of the ghetto. It was the only scrap of nature left to us. Beside it ran a path to an old hut, set away from the rest of the ghetto buildings like an afterthought. I knew the hut well. My friend Gina lived there with her daughter, who had been born the same day in the same maternity hospital as my Zygmund. In the days since I had learned of his death I would come down the path and spend time with Gina, sharing bits of food with her and her daughter. Both looked remarkably Aryan, with blue eyes and blond hair. And Gina had Gentile friends who would help. I had often beseeched her to escape the ghetto. As I walked down the path to their hut, I decided I would try once more to make them see their only chance.

As I walked down the forlorn path through the gathering darkness, I startled a young couple, who had not noticed me coming. Before I even had a chance to apologize I recognized Romek and a girl—spending their last few moments together. I hurried past without a word, and they didn't notice me.

I knocked at Gina's door and entered. Inside, Gina was busy cleaning, mending, and patching the clothes she'd picked for herself and her little girl to wear for the registration. I looked at her as though she were demented. "I'm here to say good-bye and to help you get away."

Gina looked at me blankly, so I continued. "Do you suppose for a moment you'll survive this registration business?"

"What else can I do? I look young and healthy. Maybe they'll take me on for work. We'll manage."

"You're crazy." I drew her child to me, hugging her. "Look, I've lost my child . . . you've got to save yours."

"I can't. It's too hard. And maybe my labor badge will help."

"So, you still believe in miracles after all this?" I gave up. Sadly, I kissed her and the child and left for my room.

I arrived to find the four others who shared my room also busy trying to improve the appearance of their rags and tatters.

The day was September 7, 1942. By early morning the street in front of the Judenrat was crowded. Soon it had swelled to a thousand people, milling at the periphery, pushing and pulling at the center, trying to find friends and family. There must have been several hundred mothers tightly holding the hands of their children, each taking pains to look presentable. Mothers pulled at shirttails, straightened out dresses, pasted down cowlicks, all in hopes that their children might survive by looking cute. I heard more than one mother urge her children to smile and be cheerful.

As I stood at the edge of the crowd, my eyes sought out familiar faces. Instead I saw only ghosts. Before me stood a young woman, all skin and bones, grooming herself as she held a pocket mirror to her face and rubbed a bit of red paper at her cheek. The dress she wore to look her best made me turn my head away. Next to her stood a mother trying to calm a five-year-old boy. The boy was sobbing. "Please, Mommy, let's go back to our cellar and hide with Grandma. I don't want to go to the Germans." The mother could only reply: "Behave. When Daddy comes back from the war, he'll bring you a fine toy."

Toward 7:30 in the morning, the members of the Judenrat appeared and the noise of the crowd subsided. The counselors were evidently agitated. One came forward to speak.

"Where are the elderly? Why didn't they come? If they're hiding it will go badly for them, and for the rest of us too . . . The Germans will be furious. They promised no one would be harmed. It's just a registration. Why can't you people follow orders? Why do you make our work so difficult? We're here to help, but you won't let us."

This complaint was met with silence and derision. So the Judenrat sent out the Jewish Auxiliary Police to find the missing one thousand or so that had to be in the ghetto somewhere. As tension rose, some in the crowd began to slip away, seeking their shelters after all.

At 8:00, we heard the order to line up and march out. Quietly, people begin to file out, heading for the soccer field behind the ghetto walls. There they were met by a handful of SS officers and a squad of Ukrainian militia. War-priority workers formed up in their own special group. They appeared relaxed and self-assured, as though they were untouchable. Others came to a halt in the middle of the field, eyeing them enviously. The silence was broken only by the occasional cry of a small child.

After all were assembled, Leideritz, the chief of the Kolomyja Gestapo, stepped forward. Dressed in full Gestapo regalia, with riding boots and white gloves, he motioned to a Ukrainian guard to bring the first group of Jews forward. This first group was composed of workers from the lumber mill. Leideritz motioned them all to his right. Everyone breathed easier. Next came the brick factory workers. Again Leideritz scanned the list. As he did so, his face grew red. Then he threw the list to the ground, pulled off his white gloves, and began to shout.

"Schweinehunden, who do you think you're dealing with? You can't pass off these broken-down old men as war-priority." He picked up the list and tore it into pieces. "I will make the selection." He began to move along the line, picking out the youngest and healthiest among the brick workers, sending them to the right. The rest were moved to the left by the gun butts and truncheons of the Ukrainian guards.

And so it went with group after group. By the time Leideritz had sent two thousand or more to the left, there were no illusions about what each side meant. Cries and screams filled the air as men and women were consigned to their fates, separated from one another, from children and parents. Those who begged for mercy received blows from the Ukrainians.

A mother sent to the right attempted to smuggle herself back to the left to be with her child. One of the SS officers noticed her weaving through the crowds toward the crying child. He marched into the throng, picked the child up by an arm, and carried him toward a wall. As he reached a point a meter or two from the wall he picked up the little boy, spun him over his head, and threw him at the concrete. We could see the child's brains splatter as he fell to the ground. The German turned, a leer on his face, and joined the laughter of his comrades.

I turned from this scene to see one of the Ukrainians approach

Leideritz and whisper in his ear. The commander nodded. Suddenly the selection was stopped. The SS officers took seats, and the Ukrainians fanned out among the crowd, singling out mothers and children. A bit of chalk was found and bull's eye circles drawn on the concrete wall. At the SS commander's order, the Ukrainians tore children from their mothers and carried them to the targets. And then the militiamen began target practice. At this, a hundred men broke from the crowd and set upon the militiamen. But after a few moments of firing, their bodies were added to those of the children.

I could not bring myself to believe what I had witnessed. My child had been incomparably luckier; he had died in his grandmother's arms, or so I hoped.

Near me, a young girl I knew, Joasia Singer, began attacking one of the Ukrainians, biting and kicking. "Murderer," she shrieked. "You will die a thousand deaths." The guard pinned her hands and began dragging her away from the crowd, all the while beating her with his truncheon. As she lost consciousness she was still struggling. Then another guard came over and poured water on her face so that she might revive to feel more blows. But it was too late. She had died, resisting.

When the shooting was over, many were still prostrate on the ground. The registration resumed. The next group was the wives and children of the Jewish Auxiliary Police. They seemed so sleek and healthy we could hardly look at them. We all knew that their good fortune had been bought with blood. When they formed up before Leideritz, however, a remarkable thing happened; they were all sent to the left, to death. The Jewish police members could hardly contain themselves. One stepped forward to protest: "There must be some error. These are our women and children."

Leideritz interrupted him. "Shut up. Get back to your place." No one felt any sorrow for our Jewish guards as their spirits crumpled before our eyes. As the guards stood among the saved, on the right, the others shrank from them as from lepers.

Across the field there was another small disturbance. A pharmacist had managed to cheat the Nazis by swallowing a cyanide pill. As he lay dying, others ran through his pockets hoping to find another pill.

Then it was our factory's turn. A thousand men, women, and children moved forward. First the men were to be "registered." Romek, who carried the list, handed it to an elderly worker, encouraging him to act as foreman. "Take the list. You've got a family. Maybe you'll have a better chance if you hand it over. They've been sending leaders to the right."

Why, I wondered, was Romek doing this? Did he want to sacrifice his life? To lower his own chances? My throat was too dry to scream. I did not even notice the blows of the Ukrainian truncheons moving us forward through the selection.

When Romek had reached the front of the line, Leideritz looked at him and pointed right. Romek looked the Gestapo officer in the face. "Me? To the right?"

Leideritz looked back at Romek. "No," he bellowed, "to the left. You're too slow to follow orders. And everybody behind you to the left as well."

Here again was something I could not bring myself to understand. Why had Romek not jumped to the right when he had the chance? Why had he stood there provoking the German? I could understand his not wanting to live, but why hadn't he thought how much I need-ed him? He's the one who had said: "I won't leave a woman and a baby in the middle of a war." And here he was leaving me. I would not let him go. I resolved to follow him to the left.

The selection for the women from the factory began. The Ukraini-ans cursed as they tore children from mothers to be sent to the right. But mainly women were sent left. "Get on, Jew-sow," the Ukrainians prodded us. Others continued to try to look their best. I no longer wanted to pass. I had to join Romek. I moved forward in a daze, my head down, when suddenly I felt the sting of a cat-o'-nine-tails across my legs. I looked up and found myself before Leideritz.

His leer was frightening, and he began to shout. "Goddamn Jew-ess. You're trying to make yourself look bad. Well, there's lots of life left in you. And lots of work. To the right!" The guard standing next to Leideritz shoved me toward the living.

I felt as though I had been sentenced to death. How could it be? I was to be saved, and Romek killed, when I was older, weaker, far less useful. Desperately I began to think of how I could get them to change their minds. I gathered myself together and stepped up to Leideritz.

"I beg you, let me go left. I can't be separated from my brother."

A guard stepped forward and I felt his boot in my stomach kicking me back to the right. As I lay on the ground, I could hear the Gestapo chief ranting: "You'll live, damn you. I'll decide on life or death here."

I rose and, standing among the living, searched the crowd on the left for Romek. Our eyes met, and soon Romek was moving through the crowd, seeking a way of joining me on the right. In the confusion of the selection, he got closer and closer . . . until a Ukrainian saw him making his way into a line for selection and clubbed him in the face. As Romek lay on the ground, unable to rise, I tried to break out of my group to go to him. Before I had taken a step I was felled by the truncheons.

When I regained consciousness sometime later, I found myself inside a building, and a familiar face was faintly smiling at me. It was Nunek Najder, the husband of my friend from the factory, Mati. He helped me to my feet and steadied me. Then he began to tell me what had happened.

"There were only about three hundred of us on the right when they finished the selection. We were marched here to this school building.

"You gave us a lot of trouble, Blanca. If we'd left you, the Germans would have shot you where you lay. So, I carried you over my shoulder, and the rest crowded around to hide you."

I looked at him without much appreciation. "What happened to the others, the seven thousand on the left?"

"They were told to strip and take off their shoes. Then the Germans searched their clothes for valuables and work cards. I guess it's the end for them."

Around us I could hear the sorrowful murmuring of those lucky few who had been saved. Nunek was still speaking. "I guess my wife and the other women in our family were lucky. They stayed hidden. Just the men in the family came out, five of us. Only my father-in-law and I made it. The rest were sent to the left."

"But you all had work cards, no?"

"That's true, but you saw what happened." I nodded, too tired to think about it anymore. Suddenly there was a shriek.

"Look toward the railway yards. They're marching the whole group there." We scrambled out into the schoolyard. There, through the fence, once more we watched the procession of the dead, searching out the faces of our loved ones, hoping for one last glimpse that would have to last an eternity. Our own Ukrainian guards made no effort to prevent us from watching. They leaned against the wall, evidently enjoying our misery.

Frantically, I looked from face to face. Had Romek made it this far?

Had he died on the selection ground? Then I saw him, limping along on the shoulder of another, amidst the thousand others. He did not see me as he passed. Blood was still flowing from the wound on his head, bandaged by a rag. I had no more tears. The blood throbbed through my forehead. And when the procession ended and the Ukrainian militia began to drive us back inside, I returned without a struggle. Why had God been so cruel? He had taken so many from me and left me with a life I no longer wanted. And then I thought about my seventeen-year-old twin brothers, still alive in a labor camp somewhere near Krakow. If I was destined to live, perhaps it was to do something to save them. But what could I do? My impotence overwhelmed me.

In the evening, the guards opened the school gates and ordered us back to the ghetto. "You're free to go." Free indeed; we no longer had anything to lose—not family, friends, or hope.

The ghetto that greeted us was a different place—empty, free at last of the stench and sight of death. The streets had been cleared of corpses and rubble. And a real silence reigned. I entered, overwhelmed by the feeling that I was walking along the rows of a cemetery.

My wanderings through the ghetto streets somehow led me back to our little room. I just looked at the closed door. Until this day, the room had been crowded with six people, all of them warm, supporting, encouraging, trying to make the struggle for survival seem worthwhile. There, in one corner was the spot where Romek sat, always with a plot of some sort. Was it only this morning that we had left for the registration? I remembered how Romek had locked the door and put the latchkey under the stair, saying: "If any of us makes it, the key is here." I reached for it without even thinking. This morning had seemed like such a long time ago.

I pushed the key into the lock and stood there for a moment. Two lines of poetry kept filtering through my head. "Here came my family / Now all are buried." The poet who had written these lines could at least point out their graves and grieve before them. I could not. There would be no markers in the Szeparowce woods or at Belzec. Only in my thoughts could I make the pilgrimage to the place their ashes would be scattered . . . why, why, why?

As I turned the key, I realized the door was already unlocked. The place had been ransacked. Nothing remained but broken bits of useless junk. Evidently the Ukrainians had been through the place in search of Jewish treasure. The few photographs I had managed to save were in shreds on the floor. I sat down and began trying to put one or two back together. It was a hopeless jigsaw puzzle.

As I sat, I called forth tears but they would not come. My heart had turned to stone. I could only think about how it had all happened. All the nights and days of slow death that stretched backwards a thousand years to that summer day in June 1941. Wolf was just a vague memory, this man with whom I had spent a half a dozen years, to whom I'd born a son. Only Romek seemed vivid, the one who had stayed and protected me and his nephew, with no thought of his own survival. I could not bring myself to care for anyone but him. If only he might survive somehow. If not, I would go through life with two deaths on my conscience—my mother dying for my son, my brother for me.

It was dark and growing cold in the room, the time of night when I could expect to hear Romek's characteristic footfall on the stairs as he returned from the factory. Suddenly, I could feel his presence, see his young troubled face, listen to his soothing words: "Don't worry, sis. We'll make it . . ." Did he ever believe it, really? In all that time, after each tragedy, he never broke down. All that time, yet his life was a brief moment.

I thought about his girlfriend, Jean. I had to find her . . . someone to share my sorrow. But where? Slowly I arose and moved to the window. The moon shone, the same moon of the night before, when we were still together. I pulled the shade. I needed the darkness to conjure up the last picture of the broken bodies lurching toward the rail yards, Romek's face standing out among them. Then the bodies began to turn and I saw them move toward me. The corpses were coming to claim me. A voice rose from them. "Why are you still alive? By what right do you remain?" I heard myself answer: "It's not my fault, I didn't want to be. I wanted to be with all of you, and with my brother." I looked among them for my brother. "Speak for me, Romek . . . explain to them." But I could not find his face, only a throng of the dead coming closer, threatening.

I was alone against them. I had to escape. On all fours I began to crawl from the room. I rose, threw open the door, and ran down the stairs into the dark of the night and the emptiness of the streets. The cool night felt fresh and I began to breathe.

I was haunted, I knew, by pain and grief. I should never have come back to our room. It was company I needed that night. I began to walk away from our building and stopped only when I could see a chink of light, glowing feebly from the house where some friends had lived the day before. Were they still alive? I made my way to the door, opened without knocking, and went in. There was a candle flickering on a table. Around it on the floor sat a group of strangers. But I was no stranger to their pain. Bodies shifted and a place was made for me.

As I sat down, someone looked toward me and spoke. "Were you there today? At the selection?"

"Yes," I whispered.

The others turned toward me, and a voice came out of the dark. "What happened, what was it like?" Now I understood. These people had kept hidden and survived. Those who had left them to register had not returned. I could not answer.

The question persisted. "You've got to tell us." The voice became insistent. "You've got to!"

"Don't make me. I beg you. Three hundred survived. The rest, seven thousand, were transported to Belzec." I would say no more.

Another voice began to tell me what had happened in the ghetto. They estimated that over one thousand Jews had been shot. Nothing more was said that night, though no one slept.

Early the next morning, I made my way to the Judenrat. There I found a crowd already gathered around a new edict, plastered to the wall over the last one. All inhabitants were to move forthwith to ghetto number one, the only ghetto left. We were allowed to bring such possessions as remained to us. Some in the crowd smiled ruefully at this clause. The regulations went on: new labor documents were to be issued; old ones were no longer valid; only those who had been selected for further work the day before were to receive new permits; anyone not bearing such a permit would be shot on sight. Thus, those who had survived by hiding were committed to underground life forever.

I walked away. The thought did not even touch me. I was beyond caring. Around me, people greeted one another, briefly embracing and then moving home to pack what little might still be worth carrying away.

Ghetto one was composed of three streets. It had housed the members of the Judenrat and others who could bribe their way in. It would soon become impossibly crowded, just as the other ghettos had been. I knew I had to hurry to find a corner somewhere for myself. Romek was no longer there to find one for us. . . . The thought held me again. And then the tears finally broke through. My body began to shake in spasms, and my wailing turned the heads of those who passed.

The next thing I remember was a hand on my shoulder, and then I was led away. The human touch made the tears flow more freely. Then a soothing voice broke in and I realized it was Nunek, Mati's husband, the one who had carried me unconscious from the selection to the school. As he led me away, Nunek made no effort to calm me.

About the time I was able to get a grip on the tears, I found myself being led up the stairs to my old room. I looked at Nunek. "Why did you bring me here? I can't stay here anymore. They've issued orders to move."

Nunek spoke quietly. "Yes, I know. We're here to collect your things. You'll move in with us, at our place in ghetto one."

"But there's nothing here for me to take. They ransacked the place yesterday." We entered and looked around. Nunek bent down and picked up some scraps of the torn pictures and a small yellow pillow. With these under his arm, we turned and left.

In a small room on one of the narrow streets in ghetto one, Mati greeted me. "Myszka"—little mouse—her husband called her. She embraced me as I entered.

They made a place for me to sleep on the floor in a corner. Against the other wall was what was left of Nunek's pharmacy. He was still working as a pharmacist outside the ghetto, and the word *chemist* was posted at the entry to the building. His work had earned him the luxury of a room to himself.

That day began the last stage of my life in the ghetto. My friends Nunek and Mati began to help me to want to live again. They fed me, gave me love, made me feel part of something again. The process began the next morning when they first urged me to go back to the factory. A new pass was secured and I headed out the ghetto gates once again. When I reached the factory, I automatically headed for Romek's desk in the office, expecting him to be there. I threw myself across the desk in despair. The Gentiles working in the office around me did not stop work or approach me. Lydia signaled them to leave. Then she came over to the desk, drew me up, and embraced me.

I regained some composure and began to talk. "You know what happened?"

She nodded. "Yes. I saw it for myself, from the window of a friend's house by the soccer field. When I saw Romek sent to the left side, I ran out. I went from officer to officer, pleading with them to change their minds." Lydia was crying. "Nothing helped." She held me again. "My loss was a great one too. He was a fine man. He saved so many . . . I loved him, his character, his goodness."

There was nothing to say. Lydia cleared her throat. "Look, you've got to get out, to escape. And I'm going to help you."

"No. I can't. I can't." I began to shake my head. But Lydia would not listen.

"I'm going to get you out. It's my duty to save as many of my people as I can." She nodded in the direction of the shop floor.

"Can't you realize, we're all dead already. We've suffered too much to be saved."

"I understand. But every life is sacred."

I shook my head. "Not mine, not anymore. If you really want to help me, ask one of your friends who works in a pharmacy to get some cyanide for me. That would be Christian charity."

Lydia stared at me, so I went on. "I promise. I'll use it only as a last resort."

"No, Blanca, suicide is a sin, no matter why you do it. I can't help you do it. But I can help you escape. Besides, you can't tell whether God hasn't destined you to survive and find happiness some day."

I rose to leave. But Lydia kept talking. "Blanca, stop. I want you to take Romek's job. Will you?"

I turned around. "Yes. I'd like that." Working in the office would be easier than the shop floor had been. And it would be a comfort to sit at my brother's desk, to use his pens and pads, his account books and invoices, instead of seeing a stranger in his place each day. "But Lydia, not today. I'll start tomorrow. I've got to get back to the ghetto now. It's still too much for me." She nodded and I left.

Back in ghetto one, walking toward Nunek and Mati's room, I heard a voice beckon me from an alley. I turned and saw a young woman, one I recognized from the factory. I entered the alley and she began to whisper.

"My father was on the cattle cars to Belzec. He managed to get out and got back here last night. He's hiding now. But he was in the car with your brother. He says he has a message for you."

"Where is he? Can you take me to him?"

Without another word she led me down the alley and across the backs of a couple of houses until we found ourselves at the basement door of a run-down building. There stood an older woman, the girl's mother, concerned about the strange woman her daughter had led in. My co-worker introduced me to her mother. "This is Blanca. Mrs. Wax, my mother. She's Romek's sister. Don't worry. We weren't followed."

I nodded. "Don't worry. I'll never tell a soul about this place."

Mrs. Wax turned and led us into a room, moved a large chest of drawers, and opened a trapdoor. I followed her down into the dark tunnel. There, by candlelight, I saw her husband. He was a man of about forty-five, lying on a makeshift bed. I was too eager for my brother's message to even ask about his own condition. I began to ask questions, one after another, without even waiting for the answers. "When did you last see him? Was he still bleeding? Why didn't he come back with you?"

The man in the bed did not immediately respond. He looked up blankly, as though he had not seen me. Slowly his mind cleared and he began to tell his story.

"They marched us down to the rail yard and pushed us into cattle cars, hundreds to each car, till there was no room to stand. Men, women, children, no air . . . the babies began to suffocate right away. People fainted, others started to scream for a drop of water.

"But there wasn't any. We knew most of us would die before we got to Belzec. Some people shoved bits of rag into their own mouths to suffocate faster.

"After we'd been moving for quite a while, I don't know how long, a couple of us found a small trapdoor in the roof. So, the stronger fellows pushed people away and made a human pyramid. Somebody climbed up and saw that the door was blocked by rusty old bars. We found a pocketknife and a nail file. So people took turns trying to saw through the bars. It took forever, and things were getting worse all the time. More people were dying and the stench was overwhelming. Finally, the bars gave way and a breeze blew into the car.

"It was Romek who finally got the bars off. He came down and started getting people to climb up and squeeze out. It was a small door and only the thinnest could make it. One by one the young people started to climb up and out.

"But after the third one climbed up and jumped off, we heard the shots begin. The guards on the roof had spotted them. Anyway, people kept climbing out. A bullet seemed a lot better than the gas chamber. That's when I went. Some of us made it to the woods around the track . . ." Mr. Wax paused and sank back on the mattress.

I leaned toward him. "And Romek? Did he try to get out? He would have been thin enough!"

Wax continued: "I guess he was. But he just didn't want to try. 'Tired of living . . . ready to die,' he said. But he told me I had to go. I had a wife and kids, he said.

"I said to him, 'Yes, but you've got a sister, no? You're still young and strong. You've got to try.' Well, he said it was no good for him. But he said if I was to escape I had to find you and tell you his last wish. You've got to escape. Get some false papers and get out. Alone, without him, you can make it. Tell the world . . .'"

The tears welled up again. So this was my brother's testament. I could ask the man in the bed nothing more. His face had turned ashen. I got up. "Thank you for this message." I gripped his limp hand, got up, and left.

I could hardly walk, my legs refused to carry me, and I was blinded by my tears. Stumbling into the night I saw—once again—my beloved brother's bleeding face, walking to his death. Flooded by fear, anger, and guilt, I kept repeating to myself and to Romek over and over again: But why? Why? My dear brother. Why do you have to die and I have to live? Why did you leave me all alone in this world? Why did you send me your legacy condemning me to live through this nightmare while you chose to die?

Then and many times through the days, months, and years that followed, I blamed myself for having caused my brother's death. How I wished I had not been so clever in "saving" him from Stalin's clutches.

Romek had lived with us during the two years of the Soviet occupation. One day in early 1940, the Soviet authorities issued an order permitting all refugees to the Soviet territories to return to western Poland. If they would just "register" with the local authorities, they were promised passes and transportation.

These refugees were young and middle-aged men (few with families) who had fled eastward during the first days of the German invasion of Poland. Many had tried to escape being drafted into the Polish army, and many had run to avoid the Nazi occupation. All found themselves in the Soviet zone of Poland and many remained homeless and jobless. Most were heartbroken about the fate of families left behind in the west. Believing the Soviet reassurances, they "registered" and made themselves ready for transport. As soon as I learned that Romek had registered, I convinced him to go into hiding. No sooner did he follow my pleading than a "guest" visited, asking for Romek and his whereabouts. This "guest" was an old friend of my husband's who had himself been a political prisoner. We were horrified that a person with his experience of injustice would allow himself to be used in a police role. He was embarrassed in front of us, and he left, assuring me that "all will blow over in a few days." All those who had registered were rounded up the next morning. They were "transported" all right, but to Siberian labor camps. Many of them survived the war, but my brother was not among them. (The Soviet authorities later justified their maneuver on the grounds that they needed to find out whether these refugees from the west could be trusted to become loyal citizens of the Soviet Union. Those who chose to be in Hitler-occupied territories instead of the Soviet state were obviously "enemies of the state.")

A few months later, Romek, along with many other young men, was called up for the draft. Again, I was petrified that he would end up in the Soviet army and that I would lose him. So once again I used all of the contacts my husband and I could find, and I was able to "save" him. Then came the day the Soviets started to withdraw from our city, and many people ran eastward with them. But not Romek. "I won't leave a woman and child of four months in the middle of a war, and that's it." Our fate was sealed.

As I left Mr. Wax's hideout, I carried my brother's legacy and my guilt with me. The thought that he wanted me alive and that I had killed him penetrated my whole being, causing me unbearable pain. Somehow I kept walking toward the only home I had, with Mati and Nunek. And each following day, I rose and went to the factory.

Hunger was gnawing at me. I was ashamed to ask my friends Nunek and Mati to share their food, but there was no choice. They were still getting a bit from Gentile friends who worked with Nunek in the pharmacy outside the ghetto.

Each day when he returned from work we would search his face and his hands to see if he had been able to smuggle something in. There were several people depending on him for survival: his wife; her parents; her sister Frania, just recovering from typhoid; Frania's three-year-old son, Leszek; her older sister Cyla Goldstein; and Cyla's fifteen-year-old son, Menek. Both sisters had lost their husbands in the September Action. Altogether, there were many mouths to feed. Menek had already become an expert in food smuggling. I felt lucky to be part of this family.

One day Nunek came home bleeding from wounds sustained in a beating by a Ukrainian ghetto guard. He had tried to smuggle in a bit of barley grain for the family. The "food" was torn away and a beating followed for good measure. Under these circumstances, it was especially difficult for me to share what Nunek could smuggle in. I also knew that my sharing in meager food supplies would deprive Leszek.

The boy often whimpered his complaints of hunger. He would lie on the floor, his big brown eyes full of fear, a thumb planted in his mouth, clutching the shreds of a security blanket that went everywhere with him. Though he was only three, he seemed to realize the dangers his family faced.

Our fortunes improved a bit when Mati was given a job in the community kitchen, doling out the daily ration of soup. This position allowed her to bring home rations of thicker soup, full of roots and vegetable leaves. We could eat our portions at home without first waiting in long lines.

At the factory, the few survivors moved about the floor listlessly with scant hope, their faces drawn by hunger and pain. Yet they were the lucky ones, with labor cards that assured their temporary survival.

Occasionally SS officers appeared at the factory to secure a sweater or two for shipment back to family members in Germany. Their well-fed, polished appearance unnerved us.

One of these officers, a younger one, came back to the factory repeatedly, each time taking away a pile of sweaters. These goods were not to be entered in the ledger, and I had to juggle the books accordingly. Lydia received him in the office, and I could hear their conversations. He was from Vienna, he told her, a man of culture, with a wife and two children who looked forward to his gifts from occupied Soviet Union. One day the young officer came into the office while I was alone. His glance moved from my face to my arm band with its Star of David. "You silly little bitch. You don't need to wear that. Why, with your looks you could just melt into the Aryan race without a trace. You're just killing yourself here. Why don't you get away . . . "

I just turned from him. He picked up his package of sweaters and departed. I was shaken. As I sat there thinking about what he had said, I realized that I would be late for my ration of soup unless I got back to the community kitchen right away.

As I hurried toward the ghetto gates, I saw a pair of SS men coming through them. I was desperate to avoid them, but I had to get my soup. Instead of standing aside, I decided to rush through the gates. As I did so, I brushed against one of them. Frightened, I did not look back, but began to run.

"Halt," came the order. I stopped and looked around, as though it were someone else they were summoning back. Then I turned back to the officers and found myself looking down a gun barrel. So it would end like this, I thought. Instead of shooting immediately, the German began to harangue me. "Goddamn Jewess. How dare you go through those gates before us? Subhuman excrement. Grovel . . . get down on your knees." I fell to my knees, looking to the ground. I could feel the cold steel of the gun barrel and I heard the hammer engage.

But instead of a shot, I then heard the voice of the young Viennese officer. "Let the Jew-sow go . . ." I looked up and saw him tugging at the other man's arm. "We've got too much to do today to bother with this crap." The other officer holstered his gun and they walked away.

Again, I had survived. I rose unsteadily and walked to the kitchen. As I came through the back door I found Mati, ladling out the last of the day's rations. She handed me a bowl of "thick" soup but I was too unnerved to eat.

Early the next morning, while it was still dark, we were awakened by a knocking at the window. It was Nunek's brother, Celek. Celek, although a member of the Jewish Auxiliary Police, retained a strong bond of loyalty to his brother.

We let Celek in and he began to confer with Nunek in hushed tones.

"What's wrong?" Mati asked the question that was on everyone's lips.

"It's another Action," Celek answered.

"How do you know?"

"We know. They always tell us ahead of time. So we can save our own families. Anyway, the Action's going to be in the morning, before the workers can leave for their factories. I'm going to get my wife out of the ghetto tonight. We have a hiding place on the Aryan side. Nunek, you and Mati can come along. But we've got to leave now."

"You've got to take everyone." Nunek gestured at the rest of us.

"Impossible. I only risk my neck for family."

"Well, I won't leave without my family," replied Mati.

"Suit yourself." Celek turned and left.

We began to dress, and Mati went to wake her parents and tell them the news. Then we all headed for our bunker, built sometime before by two men who had already been deported. It was a particularly good hiding place, for it led to a boarded-up storefront on the Gentile side, beyond the ghetto walls. Nunek had found a key to the store, so it might provide an escape route if discovery became imminent—unless, of course, the Germans were to post Ukrainian guards outside the ghetto walls.

Nunek was the last one to come down the ladder into the bunker. He had moved a heavy commode over the entry as far as he could. We sat in total darkness, holding hands. There were fifteen of us. The children were old enough so that we had no fear of them breaking silence and giving us away. Even Leszek understood that he could not even let a whimper escape as he sat in his mother's lap.

We could not tell when the dawn came up, but soon the sounds of shots and screams filtered down into our hiding place. Then there were loud German voices above our heads, followed by the sound of breaking furniture, window glass shattering . . . and then the bark of dogs.

Had they smelled our hiding place? If so, we were finished. I held Mati's hand tightly and whispered to her. "It'll just be the end of our suffering, that's all." Minutes passed and suddenly it became quiet again. And then we could hear sounds from the storefront side, German and Ukrainian voices. "Let's break it open." "Yeah, maybe some lousy Jew's hiding in the store." Then came the noise of a gun butt hammering at the door. So, we would be found from the Gentile side. But the door held against the pounding, and suddenly the guards were distracted. Shots were fired, and then there were screams. We heard one of the voices again. "We got him. Thought he could worm out over the wall." "Lucky you saw him. He could have gotten away." The Ukrainians lost interest in our door.

We began to smell smoke. The ghetto had been set on fire. We had to get out. There was no choice. Nunek climbed up to the trapdoor and pushed the commode aside. A few moments later he climbed back down and reported. "Our building's all right. It's not wood. But the others are burning fast. The Germans seem to have gone."

We climbed out and walked into the courtyard. There we found several corpses. The fires were putting themselves out. This time, there was no wind to fuel the flames. People were already milling about in the streets. No one gave much thought to material losses. It was friends and family that mattered. As the count of survivors was made, it became clear that there were only a few hundred left in the ghetto out of the thirty thousand Jews herded into the Kolomyja ghettos since the war began.

One morning when I arrived at work, Lydia called me into her own office, closed the door, and locked it.

"Sit down, Blanca. Look, I haven't wanted to burden you till now. But before the September Action, Romek made me swear I would help you to escape if he didn't survive.

"I tried to get you to do it without bringing my promise to him into it. But you wouldn't listen. Now it's not up to you anymore. It's my own peace of mind that's at stake. I can't sleep anymore, just thinking about it. When I do get to sleep, I have these horrible nightmares. It's Romek, all skin and bones, pointing his finger at me, saying, 'You promised, you promised.'

"I won't let you die. I gave my word on the Blessed Virgin . . . and on my affection for your brother."

Despite myself, I found myself listening to her plan. I had no desire to live. I had lost too much. But I could no longer stop her.

The next day Lydia brought me a birth certificate. It was in the name of a Ukrainian Catholic girl named Bronislava Panasiak. It had come from Lydia's brother, a Catholic priest. "You'll leave today. Now. By the next train," she insisted.

"But I can't just walk to the station. I'll be caught before I've gone a hundred meters. They'll just shoot me. Besides, I have no money. I'll be alone. How can I leave now?"

"I've thought of all that. My brother-in-law will walk you to the station. You'll go to Lwów. I've got a sister there you can stay with. I've already told her you're coming.

"Once you're away from here you'll recover. With your looks, your languages, and your new identity, you'll make it.

"Besides, there are others at the factory planning to escape. They can help."

"Who?" I asked.

Lydia took me to the door and pointed out a man working nearby. "Him, for example."

I walked over to the man and began to question him. Yes, he was planning to get out. He'd been a businessman and had a fair amount of money and gold still hidden. "It's all hidden at the bottom of a well on my property. Lydia is going to help me get it. I'll share some of it with her. I'm getting out while there's still a chance."

I could not tell him that he had no chance. His Polish was heavily accented with Yiddish and would give him away instantly. I returned to the office.

"All right, I'll do it." I took the birth certificate. "But not today. Soon, very soon."

When I got back to the room I told Nunek and Mati. They were unanimous.

"You've got to go. And soon." Nunek was particularly urgent. "When you get settled in Lwów, send word through my friends at the pharmacy. We'll join you." Mati looked doubtful, but Nunek persisted. "Don't worry. I'll convince her."

The next day I went to work. Two days later I told my friends that I would not be heading back to the ghetto after work that night. As my friends left I told them not to worry about me. They wished me luck.

After closing, Lydia took me to the office of a Gentile physician with whom I'd left some of Wolf's medical equipment and a microscope before I went into the ghetto. I wanted to sell all of this to him and I asked whether he would be interested in buying the whole lot. Angrily he consented and threw at me fifty zlotys—a fraction of its value. In parting he remarked sarcastically that it was quite a miracle that I was still alive. "After all, everyone knows that your husband was a Communist." Naturally, I did not tell this "good" doctor that I was about to run away from the ghetto into the Aryan side.

I slept in the factory that night, waking repeatedly in a sweat from dreams that foretold the dangers ahead. The next morning was my last in the factory. The day passed slowly. When darkness fell, Lydia's brother-in-law appeared. She introduced us, and he asked me to call him by his Christian name, Adam. "After all. We're going to be old friends tonight."

Lydia embraced me. "There's nothing to worry about. Everything is going to be all right." She pulled the Star of David off my sleeve.

Arm in arm, Adam and I left the factory and headed for the station. Adam was voluble, animated, as though he had not a care in the world, though we both knew he was risking his life for a stranger. Walking on the sidewalk made me feel light-headed, but Adam held my arm firmly. As we walked along, I kept repeating to myself, "My name is Bronislava Panasiak. I was born on December 4, 1915. My parents' names were . . . , they were born on . . . , in the province of . . . " It was the end of October 1942.

8

Lwów

The train gathered momentum. I had made it through the station undiscovered and was on my way to "freedom." It was still dark, dark as my confused thoughts and feelings. Curling up in the corner of the compartment, I turned my face toward the window, my eyes trying to pierce the darkness. Darkness was my friend, a blessed solace I wished could last forever. Thoughts succeeded each other rapidly: what about tomorrow? What will happen? Will I survive in this city I've never been to? Why am I fleeing the comfort of a certain death for the unknown? What have I left behind in the town where those I loved lived and died? No. I can't allow myself to think about them now. I had to think about the new person I had become.

Who was I? Bronislava Panasiak! I was born in Lwów, I'm Greek-Catholic, twenty-five years old, and . . . and all alone in the world . . . This last at least I wouldn't have to rehearse as I tried to force myself into the mind of the woman I was to impersonate. I had to obliterate the person I was, get out of myself and into someone else. I kept repeating this as if it would help the transformation. I was now an Aryan, with a right to life, and no longer a Jewess, hunted like prey. I was again a human being, not a number on an arm band. It was hard to come to terms with these truths, to learn the terms of a free life. I had forgotten how to be free, to act normally, to tread the sidewalks instead of the gutter, to look people in the eye without baring my fears. My heart beat so strongly I feared it would betray me. At the same time, my conscience kept reminding me that indeed I was a traitor, fleeing from a cause. I tried to construct a defense. Death was no cause that demanded loyalty, and death, by gas or bullet, was the only reward. I had to live . . . to tell the world. "Ha . . . what chance of life do you have? How naive," replied the saboteur inside. But there was no way back. I had to put an end to this inner turmoil. Whether or not I perished on the Aryan side of existence, I had to compose myself, to wear a mask of calm indifference over my troubled features.

The grey dawn of a new day began to overcome the blackness outside. A few passengers stirred, woke, and turned to survey their new traveling companions. How was I to avoid their attention? A side glance revealed a German passenger, busying himself with his bag. I had to be able to look him in the eye, without trepidation. Yet I was scared, scared of the daylight, the passengers, and so very scared of my new life.

The train slowed as it approached a station. The sign read Lwów. It was a city I knew nothing about, but I could make no inquiries. There was nothing to do but join the surging mass of people funneling through the station underpass to the street. My knees seemed to lock beneath me, my step was unsteady. I carried myself up to the window of a large store and began to survey the latest fashions with lively interest, trying desperately to regain my balance. Where, I began to ask myself, does this flood of immobilizing fear come from? I had rehearsed everything so well; I knew who I was now, and no one looking at me could see the Jewess escaped from the ghetto. Unless, that is, I revealed myself through my nerves. Cautiously and furtively I surveyed the square. It came to me suddenly that the large open plaza, the wide streets emerging from it were the cause of my fear. I had to learn once again to walk them with ease and confidence. For two years I had passed among the narrow darkened lanes and alleys of the ghetto, pushing and jostling just to avoid the cadavers covering footpath and gutter. Here I was among humans again, walking in comfort and with a purpose.

The window displays seemed lovely to me, the houses spacious, the cars and trams almost beyond my imagination. Little wonder that I needed time to find my feet and take hold of life again. From Hades to the metropolis was too long a step.

Having come to grips with my uncertainty and fear, I slowly began to step in with the passersby, going somewhere, anywhere. I came to a tram stop, got aboard one, and began to search out the street signs, trying to remember Lydia's instructions. My voice was still too un-steady to ask anyone for directions, but I managed to find a stop close to my destination. Clutching my letter of introduction, I made my way to a large building where Lydia's sister and her family lived. Again, fear gripped me: what if they won't have me? What if they are away? Where will I go? If only they let me stay awhile and get my bearings, I might be able to fill the role of the woman I was supposed to be. I sud-denly felt sure I could make it. I climbed the stairs, and suddenly I was at the apartment, ringing the doorbell.

I thought I was dreaming as Carola and Robert, Lydia's sister and her husband, greeted me cordially and ushered me in. Both were pre-pared for my arrival.

For two weeks I stayed inside, too frightened to leave the house. My host and hostess reassured me that I looked my part perfectly, and no one would suspect me. With my blond hair braided into a crown, I was assured that I looked just like a German Fräulein or a Slavic peasant girl. I had to break out and begin moving around the town establish-ing a normal way of life. All I had to fear, they said, was the fear haunt-ing my eyes and the sadness of my demeanor. "You look like you've just come from a family funeral." Exactly! I didn't know it then, but it was that fear and the funereal air that continued to give me away in the years that followed.

In fear of leaving the apartment, I kept giving excuses. By the sec-ond week I began to notice a change in the house. It was becoming clear that my new friends wanted to get rid of me. Whether their neigh-bors had warned them of the dangers of hiding me or whether it was that I could not afford to pay them, I never learned. But they made their discomfort evident enough. I had to leave; I had to stand on my own feet.

I began again to take stock of my position. I was by nationality a Ukrainian woman, but I didn't know the language. So I had to decide on my own origins. I decided to be a Polish woman, child of a Ukrai-nian father. I left Carola and Robert's place and began searching for new shelter. I was too new at the game to realize that my tracks had to be covered. So stupidly I began looking for something in the same apartment block. I succeeded in my very first inquiry, renting a room in the home of the superintendent of a place around the corner from theirs. After paying two months' rent and security, I still had a few zlo-tys left. I knew I couldn't hang around my new quarters all day, but had to pretend to go out to work. So every morning I left and returned only after working hours. After seven days of exploration, my landlord reminded me I needed a registration certificate from the local police precinct to remain where I was legally.

I had no idea what traps police stations held for Jews with false papers. Standing for hours in long lines, applicants were thoroughly scrutinized by the "Szmalcownicy"—Polish specialists in the identification of Jews on false identity papers. (*Szmalcownicy* comes from the word *smalec,* which means *fat, grease,* or *lard*—hence it carries the implication of fattening up.) The extortionists hung around, as ready to blackmail as to turn one in to the Gestapo. Paying off these experts became a regular feature of my new life. Unaware of these dangers, I went along, filled out the forms, and completed my registration without a hitch. I began to feel more in control of my life and started to think about work.

The day after registering, I went to see Carola and Robert, hoping they might have some advice about job hunting. I was met at the door by their maid, who informed me coldly that the couple had left town and she didn't know when they'd be back. Behind her I heard a door in the flat close with a thud. I knew where I stood.

Some days later, as I sat alone in my room I heard a loud knock on my door. I opened it thinking my landlord was coming for a chat, but instead there stood Anthony Lieberman, from the factory in Kolomyja. Lydia had helped him retrieve gold from his old home after his escape from the ghetto, and now he had made his way to Lwów, in the company of an Aryan he had paid well. The guide had left him at the station, and now Anthony had nowhere to turn. He had found my address through Carola. Now my fears joined his. What if his guide had followed him? The last thing I needed was any connection with a Jew. I explained my fears and asked him what he intended to do. Bewildered, he had no idea beyond staying the night, if I would let him. He had, he said, a contact, a liaison for "Aryan-Jewish affairs" who would settle him with a place and documents, for a price. Frightened as I was, there was nothing to do but say yes. It was too late to turn him out.

We spent the night at the table, talking about the past and future. In the morning, Anthony pulled himself together, expressed his thanks, and got up to leave. At that very moment, the landlord broke into the room and began to shout. "What a story. The maid where you were staying has just told me what's been going on here. A couple of Jews on false papers. How dare you, risking the lives of innocent Christian people, running away from the ghetto where you belong, hiding among us. It's just too much . . . a thousand zlotys right now or you'll be in the streets and I'll be on my way to the Gestapo." Having delivered himself of his indignation, he stood there, scowling at us. I began to feel faint, blood draining from my head. Anthony began to argue, but I reached for my purse and handed over five hundred zlotys—it was all I had. The landlord grabbed it and held out his hand for the rest. Anthony handed it over, but it wasn't enough. We had to leave right away. I picked up my few things and was in the street a few minutes later, ushered out by the landlord's abuse. We moved quickly along the street, trying to lose ourselves in the crowd.

Suddenly, as we turned a corner, I saw a quiet public garden dotted with inviting benches. I felt my feet give out as I reached the nearest bench. What were we to do? Fighting to survive would be too hard. I should never have left the ghetto and Kolomyja. Anthony said there was no way out but to contact the "liaison."

Without much difficulty we found his place. We were received by a suspicious-looking man in a darkened room. He looked like a Jew himself. Sitting in silence while Anthony talked to him, I wondered whether he too was on false identity papers, making his living in "liaisons." After much whispering and the exchange of a wad of bills, the stranger left the flat. I shared my uneasiness with Anthony, warning that the whole business might be a trap. Here I sat, no money, no hope, and willpower to fight draining away.

An hour later our liaison returned, telling Anthony that he had located a small place in the German section of town. The lady who owned it was "volksdeutsch," ethnic German, and no one would expect Jews to hide in the most dangerous section of the city. All we needed was two hundred zlotys. "This place is worth millions," he insisted. "It's right across from Gestapo headquarters."

We were back on the street, with a new address. But I couldn't just tag along with Anthony. He was a total stranger to me. I didn't have a penny and couldn't check into a hotel. "Can you lend me some money, Anthony?"

He gave me an embarrassed look and began to speak quietly but earnestly. "Look, I know I've lost you all your money. So why not come with me. There'll be room for both of us till you get your bearings. Sure, I'll lend you something, but meanwhile, come with me. You mustn't take offense. Consider it my way of returning your help. At least stay the night."

Touched by his earnestness and respect, I still hesitated. Would it be even more dangerous for us together? Anthony insisted. He would introduce us as cousins. "Come now, we can't worry about conventions." What I couldn't tell him was that it was more dangerous for me to be with him than alone, for he bore a visible mark of Jewishness and I did not. But seeing the tears in his eyes, I relented.

The small apartment—two rooms and a kitchen—turned out to be quite comfortable, and we settled in together. Anthony wouldn't leave the place at all, however. His Polish just carried too heavy a Jewish accent. But I began to feel free to move around town, marketing and setting up house. Overnight with Anthony turned into a couple of weeks of keeping house together. I even managed to make contact with Mati and Nunek through an Aryan acquaintance. I wanted to convince them to escape as I had. Nunek would insist on his wife getting out first. I sent them my address and began to look forward to Mati's arrival. I started thinking about setting up house together, starting to look for work, and building up some independence. I felt sorry for Anthony. He needed a "front" so badly, but he had both money and gold, and my safety rested on getting away from him. I would leave him with gratitude, but also with the sense that I did as much for him as he did for me.

And then I remembered someone who could help me. Before the Kolomyja ghetto had been liquidated, I had learned of a successful escape. The man who had gotten away was an old friend of ours, Edward Rothman. He had been married to a Gentile, who, as a German, had been allowed to divorce. She had done so for the sake of their child. But she had managed to continue to help and protect him. Edward was living in a small town not far from Lwów under false identity papers as Stanislau Glac. He was working in a government office.

I tried hard to recall the address he had passed back to the ghetto and wrote to him, hoping I had remembered it right. His answer came back almost immediately. Overjoyed at my escape, he promised to visit me the next week. To see a familiar face would be a delight. Besides, with his contacts, Edward would be able to help me find work.

The Tuesday morning I expected him, our landlady came to the door. "There's someone to see you." I rushed out expecting to see a bewhiskered, disguised Edward. Instead I found a stranger, who pushed me aside and entered the apartment. My first thought was that this was some friend of Anthony's. But one look at Anthony showed that he didn't recognize our visitor either. The stranger, however, seemed to have made no mistake. He beckoned me into the room and locked the door. "Dear lady," he began, "as we both know, you are a Jew escaped from the Kolomyja ghetto, here on false identity papers." He drew a card from his coat. "And as a Gestapo agent I have the duty to arrest you."

Instead of fear, I felt fury. "That's all rubbish. Your information is all wrong."

The stranger calmly replied: "If the lady wants more information, I'll be happy to supply it. You, madam, are the wife of a physician who joined the Soviets, and you, Mr. Lieberman, are quite well fixed financially . . . a man one can do business with."

The game was up. Our tormenter had his facts right. But where had he gotten them? Lydia's sister, her maid, the landlady? No time for guessing now. Edward was on his way, and he was going to walk into this trap too. We had to get out of the house before Edward arrived. I took my coat off the rack and urged Anthony to do likewise. But our visitor remained motionless. He began to tell us what it was like to fall into the Gestapo's hands. "They're particularly nasty with Jews who've tried to get away." He carried on with his gruesome descriptions, but we were not really listening. He forced us to dress and move out of the apartment. As I laced my shoes, he informed me that I needn't be so thorough. "You have no one to impress and not very far to go. Gestapo headquarters is across the street, you know. So get a move on, Jew-bitch."

Outside it was a cold December day, and I paid more attention to bundling up than to his threats. Death didn't matter anymore; it was the torture we faced. When we were finally ready to go, our stranger became a bit mellow. He turned back to the room and slumped in a chair. In a whisper, he started to talk.

"You know, dear sir and madam, beneath this Gestapo officer's chest beats the heart of a Polish patriot, one sensitive to human suffering. I'd really like to save you both. For one thousand zlotys, you can both go free . . ." He fell silent, and then stammered: "Everybody's got to make a living you know."

Suddenly we were back on safe and familiar ground again. An extortionist, though admittedly a well-informed and assured one. I couldn't face this "sensitive" Pole and turned away in disgust as Anthony counted out the zlotys he demanded. As he left, Anthony smiled graciously for the benefit of the landlady, who had sulked about the door, wondering who our first visitor had been. "Just an old acquaintance," Anthony explained. As our old acquaintance descended the last stair, Edward came through the gate and entered the apartment. He shouted warm greetings. Should I reply or pretend I didn't know him? I had no time to think; Edward advanced quickly and closed his big arms around my back. He was happy to see me alive. The extortionist took a fleeting glance at the obviously Polish behavior of this very Polish-looking visitor and turned to go, before he lost his easy pickings.

I invited Edward in and briefly explained what had just happened. His safety was in jeopardy, and I had hoped that business would have kept him away from Lwów that day. But it was a familiar story to Edward, though he seemed nervous as he tried to calm me. "Life as an Aryan," he noted, "is almost more dangerous than life in the ghetto. It's not just the Gestapo, but all those honest Poles who have made blackmail one of the country's biggest private businesses. Using their long experience of the Jews among them, they have become insects trailing scents that lead to Jews with a bit of money. While they still have any, they are safe. But penniless ones can't last, for turning them in gets the patriot a Gestapo bounty of at least fifty zlotys."

How, I wondered, could our extortionist have known so much about us?

Edward had been very lucky so far, but he had lived long enough on the Aryan side to have lost any illusions. He had lived in Kolomyja with his German wife, Kate. After the German occupation began, she had hid Edward and then left with him for Lwów, where she set him up in a respected position and where he acquired a wide circle of friends. Edward looked the part of the Polish aristocrat, with a noble demeanor and an elegant mustache.

Edward began to advise us. First we must leave this place as soon as we could. Our extortionist would be back soon or would send another member of his team. "These people will milk you till you're dry and then throw you to the Gestapo."

"But if we move, won't he just find us again?"

"There's always the chance," Edward agreed. "Everyone in the city must register with the police. It's easy for them to check the records. I'll bet your visitor got his dope from the liaison for Aryan-Jewish Affairs."

"Maybe we should go to Warsaw," I suggested. "Start over in a larger city."

Edward agreed. "But first you've got to get out of here." He gave me the address of some friends where I could spend the night without registering. "Tell them Mr. Glac sent you." It would be a place to relax for a day before starting for Warsaw. "Now, let's go for a walk, Blanca. It will do you good."

As we walked, I told Edward my dilemma. He was right; I had to leave Lwów. But I was expecting Mati. I had given her my address and I feared that she was already on her way. She would be walking into a trap. Edward agreed to find her and send her on to me. "Whatever you do, don't write to your friends in the ghetto about your problems. It will just scare them out of trying to get out of Kolomyja themselves. Any delay now will cost them their lives. The news from Kolomyja is very bad. Your luck here hasn't been too good. Does Anthony have a really large hoard of money? What sort of contacts has he made?"

After I told Edward the whole story, he turned to me earnestly. "Look you've got to get to Warsaw, you've got to go alone and start out fresh there. With your looks, your intelligence, your Polish, you can make it." He reached into his pocket and pulled out two hundred zlotys. "I expect this loan back after the war. Don't go back to Anthony. All his money can't help him. He should have never tried to leave Kolomyja. Hiding with some Gentiles he could pay off would have been much better for him."

By the time we parted it was late afternoon. I went home to pack and then took Anthony to the address Edward had given us. The next morning we boarded separate cars on a train for Warsaw.

9

Warsaw

My first month on the Aryan side had not been good. I left Lwów with a heavy heart and even less hope than when I had arrived.

As I rode to Warsaw, the others in the train compartment talked about nothing but Jews on the run. Of course I was not bold enough to join the conversation, so I just leaned back and pretended to nap, all the while straining to catch every word.

"It's horrible, what they're doing with the Jews. I live near the ghetto in Lwów, and I can't bear it. They're just going too far, and the Lord will avenge himself on them one day."

"That's rubbish," replied a man across the way. "Dear lady, they deserve everything they get. Those damn Yids reigned over us as if they owned the whole country. They took the bread from our children's mouths, they got fatter and sleeker at our expense for years. And now they're trying to worm their way into the Gentile world, buying their way with their wealth, subverting good Poles to save their skins."

A teenage boy joined in. "The Germans think they've rounded them all up, but they're wrong. I just found one, a girl and her five-year-old brat, in my neighbor's place. So I called the cops. What did she do? She tried to bribe them with a big ring off her finger. Didn't work, though. They hauled her off to the Gestapo, and the kid too."

The discussion became more general. Some reported seeing incidents themselves; others knew about them only from hearsay. Some expressed pride in their collaboration with the authorities. Any sign of regret was ridiculed.

My thoughts moved on to the matter of survival in this hostile world. Maybe I could find some corner of Polish society, true Poles like those I knew before the war, who would understand that Poland's enemies were the Germans, not the Jews.

As the train pulled into Warsaw, my mood was no better. True, it was a city I'd lived in for more than a year back in the thirties, so I knew my way around. But I had no idea where to turn. I pulled my suitcase off the rack and walked down the platform and into the street. Anthony, who had been riding in another compartment, met me there. As we walked away from the station, I felt we were being followed. Was it an illusion? No, Anthony felt it too. I told him to keep walking, not to look around or to change his pace.

What was happening? I couldn't help thinking, "Is there a mark of Cain on our foreheads?" After a couple of blocks, we found a small hotel and registered. The desk clerk showed us to a room, but whatever calm I had mustered was already shattered. I slipped out of the place by the back entrance and came around to the front.

There they were, one at the hotel entrance, two lounging across the street. I began to walk down the street, looking for a cafe with a phone, so I could call Anthony and warn him. Suddenly, the three men broke off the stakeout and walked away. Maybe they'd decided that we weren't game after all.

Since the hotel wasn't safe, we checked out and began heading down Marszalkowska Street. "Lets try a bigger, posher hotel," I suggested. "Maybe it will be safer." Without any further trouble, we ended up with two nice rooms in a large place on Moniuszki Street. As transients, we were permitted to stay three days without police registration. After that we had to find a contact—someone to help us secure a safe place to stay and to provide us with false registration slips.

A name came to me. My host in Lwów, Lydia's brother-in-law, had said something about a Ukrainian underground organization with a liaison in Warsaw. Somehow I managed to remember the name and address. I felt I had to use this contact, even though I had no idea of the group's aims, objectives, methods, or politics. I had to tread lightly and feel the situation out. Getting the man's address was no problem, since it was a law office listed in the phone directory.

I introduced myself as a Pole of Ukrainian background, just as my identity card said. The lawyer was willing to see me.

"What can I do for you?" he asked as I sat down.

"I am here on a political mission," I began. "I can't really talk about it. You understand, sir, don't you? But I need a room for a couple of days, a safe one."

"I understand. Here's the address of a pretty safe place. It's across the Vistula in the Praga District. A widow's place."

I looked at the address. It was a district I knew, in a working-class part of Warsaw, full of taverns, brothels, and other places of doubtful repute. But it would probably do for us. I thanked the man and left.

Anthony and I moved in. The old widow asked no questions. My introduction through the Ukrainian contact was good enough for her. As in Lwów, Anthony settled down and kept off the streets while I made the rounds. Our landlady was a simple, warm-hearted woman who suspected nothing. In fact, she sorrowfully told me about the atrocities committed by the Germans in the ghetto. "I'm horrified. I'd like to help the Jews, but I'm scared. Lots of people have been shot for hiding them." I grew to like this woman a great deal and regretted that we had to deceive her.

Once our stay extended beyond the few days originally agreed upon, the widow asked for our registration slips from the police station. I knew we couldn't expose ourselves to the dangers of registering in person. I went back to the Ukrainian liaison.

"I've got a problem," I explained. "My mission is too dangerous to expose myself, but I've got to get false police registrations. Can you arrange it?"

"I know just the man." The lawyer made a quick phone call. "I've set up an appointment for tomorrow. All you need are your documents and enough for a payoff." He gave me an address. Though I couldn't know from looking at it, the place bordered the ghetto wall. I was too ignorant to be frightened.

The next day, we met our contact and made the deal. It was simple, brief, and expensive. Fortified with police registrations, Anthony and I quickly headed back toward the tram stop. As we turned a corner, a vast wall reared up before us. There was the ghetto. Fear chilled my body. Looking around, I realized that this was the worst place to be stopped, especially for a man. There were too many snoops lurking around. In fact, within moments a gaggle of street urchins appeared, shouting after us. "Where's your arm bands, Yids?" I kept walking, but Anthony turned toward them. He pulled a couple of the kids into an alley. I guessed he was giving them a bit of money to lay off. I supposed that he would try to meet me at home or at the Ukrainian lawyer's office. So I kept moving down the street.

Without thinking, I mounted the first tram that came along and rode around for hours. No one seemed to take any notice of me. After a while the neighborhood began to look familiar. Soon I saw that the tram was passing the Ukrainian lawyer's office. I got out, hoping Anthony would be there. To my relief, he was waiting in front of the office, looking pale and exhausted. We headed home.

I realized then how different everything was when I was not with Anthony. Sitting in that streetcar, no one had paid any attention to me; I just faded into the scene, looking like any average Polish girl. With Anthony, I always drew a crowd. Edward's advice came back. Anthony could only put me at risk. I had to try to make it alone. The problem was how to break it to Anthony.

"Look, Anthony, this is a war of nerves we're in and we'll both do better alone than we could together. I'll help you all I can, but I've got to try it on my own." He seemed to be listening, but he didn't want to hear.

"No, with my money we have a good chance."

I tried again. "The money can help you, and thank God you've got it. But you've got to let me go." There was no reply.

I'd become a bundle of nerves with Anthony. I had to start working, to fight for my bread and my existence. Becoming Bronislava Panasiak was going to take time and stamina. It was a goal, a challenge, something I could hang on to. But it would take all my strength.

One morning a couple of days later, I left our room, police registration in hand, and set out for the public employment office—the Arbeitsamt. After standing in line for an hour or so, I found myself in front of the clerk, asking what sort of work was available. I was in luck. A salesgirl was needed at a large German-owned department store, Manfred Milke Co., right in the heart of fashionable Warsaw—Nowy Swiat, the new world. The clerk told me to report there the next day.

Next I needed a roof over my head. Through the newspaper, I found a Polish family with a spare room to rent in a nice part of town. There was just one hitch. The place was on Graniczna Street, right across from the ghetto. I went to look the place over anyway. The room itself was fine. The owners seemed intelligent enough and entirely unsuspecting. Perhaps living alone close to the ghetto would be safer after all. No Jew would be brazen enough to live in this part of town. The lady of the house asked me a couple of questions: Do I go out a lot? Will I want to use the kitchen? She was relieved to hear that I'd take my meals in the workers' canteen at the store, and I didn't expect to use the kitchen. It was a good deal for her.

I moved in and began to feel like a Gentile girl working for a German firm in the city. A job, a room, papers—it was a good start. Now I had to help Anthony find a room. We located a good sublet on Wielka Street. He moved in, and I promised to do his shopping and visit him daily, just to be sure he wouldn't show his face and his accent on the street. He seemed to accept the arrangement.

I began to get into a new routine. Dressed in the brown smock of a Milke salesgirl, I went out of my way to avoid attracting attention. I was just one of a thousand employees, distinguished only by my name embroidered on the smock above the name of my department—school supplies. Just a cipher in the Manfred Milke empire—diligent, attentive, professional.

Every morning, the division supervisor—a rotund German—came into the department to look around. At first he didn't even notice me. So much the better. His indifference gave me confidence and I begin to raise my head, to take some notice of my co-workers. But occasionally I'd catch myself fantasizing: what if I had a link to the underground? Rumor had it that the underground was very active in Warsaw. For all I knew, my co-workers could be in it. They were a varied lot. Many had faces and manners that bespoke other places and occupations. Some led a secretive existence, befriending no one, disappearing the moment work ended, not even stopping for a snack at the store canteen or the nearby cafes. There were whispers that some were Jews on false identity papers; others were said to be in the underground. I took in the gossip, but tried to avoid getting involved. I just stuck diligently to my work.

The woman behind the counter with me was a young Pole, anti-Semitic and without intelligence, but full of gossip and stories about men. She also dwelt on the changes she'd seen in the store during the past year. She'd even seen a couple of Jews caught passing for Aryans and removed by the police, sometimes the Germans, sometimes the Poles. The details made my blood run cold. I feigned indifference and tried to change the subject. But I wondered if I could go on when every mention of a Jew in hiding immobilized me with fear? Would I ever be unaffected by such stories?

My new life was lonely. Like a robot I rose each morning, worked through the day, stopped at Anthony's for a short visit, and then went back home for a night as likely to be sleepless as not. No rest, no joy, not even a walk down the street or a couple of friends to pass the time with. These pleasures from another world were forbidden as the price of survival in the Aryan world.

The new year, 1943, approached, and the store planned a gala party for its staff in a rented hall at a fashionable hotel, the Europa. Lights, gaiety, dancing—I'd have to go or it would be noticed.

Though I played my part, inside I felt nothing but mourning. Dancing was the last thing on my mind. Knowing no one, I stood at the edges of the dance floor, watching the crowd. Then I caught sight of a lovely blond girl, Nina, from the toy department on my floor. She seemed to be about seventeen and very charming. She danced with the air of youth and freedom. I'd been told that she was engaged to a German officer, a very jealous young man. The thought repelled me, but I couldn't help admiring her grace and beauty. After a tour or two around the room, I joined a table of older women sipping punch. One of them turned an inquisitive eye toward me.

"Why aren't you dancing? You're young and pretty."

"How about you?" I replied.

My questioner subsided with a knowing smile. "We must talk sometime, you and I." There seemed to be a message in her look as she spoke. Or was I imagining things? Her gaze continued to look threatening, and I made my excuses, moving back into the milling crowds. As midnight struck, a toast was raised.

"To the victory of the great German armies. Heil Hitler."

I found another seat, my mind turning back to the Kolomyja ghetto, the Warsaw ghetto, all of the places where my brethren were now being starved, tortured, and gassed. I couldn't bear the party lights and laughter. Shortly after midnight I left, seeking a tortured peace in my room.

As I walked down Graniczna Street along the ghetto wall, people were laughing and greeting 1943 with shouts of joy. On the other side, darkness reigned. And where did I belong? My soul was locked up on the dark side of this high wall, while my body walked on this side. Just over the wall were thousands to whom the new year would bring death. What would it bring me? Would any of them survive? Would I? Would any of us be able to tell our story to the world?

I walked past a German sentry at the ghetto gate. I was so close I could almost hear him swear under his breath. Why did he have to be on duty tonight of all nights, guarding Jews who wouldn't die fast enough for the Reich?

From my room, I could see a small section of the ghetto. I stood at the window in the dark, trying to pierce the blackness below. Memories came back—misery, despair, grief, sorrow, mourning for my family. The hunger, disease, the odors of rotting flesh came back into my nostrils. I would carry the memories forever. I was condemned to them. Yet here I stood, free, while my brothers and sisters on the other side of the wall dreaded the new day. If only I could reach out and touch one of them with my real self, cry over our yesterdays and tomorrows. I'm Jewish. The words rang in my head, without passing my lips. My head was throbbing, and I started to choke. Too tired to stand, I fell into a chair, turned on a lamp, and began to write.

The words rushed out, overwhelming each other, making no sense. My thoughts could not express themselves yet. Would they ever? I tore up the pages and tried to sleep, in vain. Dawn reached into my room, a holiday, free from work. I'd have to go and visit Anthony. The poor fellow had become a shut-in.

It was a fine, crisp morning as I boarded the bus to Wielka Street. Entering the room, I was struck by Anthony's pallor and his look of fear. It was the extortionists again. They had come the night before and taken a sizeable chunk of money in exchange for a few more days of freedom. Anthony couldn't identify the thugs, but he thought they might have been sent by the man who arranged our police registrations.

"They asked about you too, Blanca. But I told them you didn't have much money so they weren't very interested. They said you weren't worth their effort."

It was only a question of time before they found me. They'd be after me the minute they'd squeezed everything out of Anthony. I should have listened to Edward's warning in Lwów: cut all ties with Anthony. But I couldn't just turn my back on another human being. What to do now? Start over? New papers, new job, new room? Another new life? Impossible. I didn't have the money to buy new documents, let alone the rest. I'd just have to take my chances. Maybe Anthony could hold off the sharks for a while, doling out bribes, but sooner or later he'd run out, and then these bloodsuckers would drag him to the Gestapo for the bounty, fifty zlotys per Jew.

After a couple of hours of comforting Anthony, I went back home, determined to cut all ties, to break the chain that otherwise would drag us both down.

On my way to work the next morning, I posted a letter to Edward in Lwów. At the corner of Graniczna Street I found a crowd transfixed by a convoy of trucks leaving the ghetto filled with Jews. As I joined the crowd someone said: "This is too much, what are they doing to those miserable creatures?"

"Where are they taking them?" asked a bystander.

"To the gas chambers at Treblinka," someone volunteered.

A rough voice intervened. "Thank god for Hitler. At least someone is getting rid of the vermin."

The trucks disappeared but the crowd lingered. I moved on and soon was at work—brown uniform, impassive countenance, the polite and helpful salesgirl. No one could see the real person inside.

Soon after lunch, two uniformed SS officers entered the store. Just shoppers, I told myself. But they headed straight for the administrative offices. A moment later they came out of the office, moving right for me. As they marched down on me, I reached for my papers, but I knew I was finished.

They came up to my station—and kept right on going, past me into the toy department. They were after Nina, the young girl with the German boyfriend. What could she have done? Surely she wasn't Jewish. She must have stolen something. But that wouldn't bring the Gestapo down on her.

As Nina left with the Gestapo, the shop floor erupted into a buzz of whispers. What did she do? Finally the store manager came out of the office. "It's all right girls, back to work. Nina turned out to be a Jewish girl on false identity papers, that's all. Please, back to work now."

Poor girl. She had perfect looks for an Aryan, and she had herself a Wehrmacht officer too. But it wasn't enough. How could I make it if she couldn't?

After Anthony's news and Nina's arrest, I was convinced the ax would fall on my head any time. A couple of days later I was approached at work by a suspicious-looking customer.

"Can I help you, sir?"

"Maybe. Can you spare me a few minutes outside?" We slipped out the side door.

"I was in a team that shook down your friend, Anthony, you know, this morning. But the other guys didn't cut me in fair. So I want you to put a word in with Anthony for me privately. Otherwise, I'll have to turn you in."

"Yes, okay." Anything to get rid of him. He left and suddenly I felt sick. I went to the supervisor and asked for the rest of the day off.

Back at home there was some good news waiting, a letter from Mati. Under a new name, Juliana Górska, she had arrived in Lwów and wanted me to write to her via Edward. My pleasure at reading her letter was short-lived. The landlady knocked at my door. Maybe she wanted to chat about the fate of the Jews across the wall my window looks down upon, I thought. But that wasn't it after all.

The old woman didn't know how to begin, but after a moment she blurted it out. "A woman from the other side of town, from Praga, came to see me today. She told me I was harboring a Jew in my home."

"Well, if you think it's true, you better tell the authorities," I replied with as much indifference as I could muster. "What an absurd allegation. Let someone try to prove it."

My landlady was taken aback. "We'll have to talk about this." She turned for the door of my room. It was all too much for me. I fell on my bed and remained there till morning. As day broke, I began to think about getting to work.

All that day, thoughts about Anthony assailed me. Right after work I ran out to see him. His room was pitch dark and he sat in the middle of it, with his arms wound around his body in a catatonic self-embrace.

The extortionists were squeezing more and more, faster and faster. Every hour there was a new face and a new threat: "Pay off, dirty Jew, or it's over." Anthony was resigned to death. He had just one money belt of gold coins and jewels left.

After a few minutes he began to speak. "I was going to give myself up this morning, but I wanted to see you once more. You've done so much for me. I can't pay you for all you've done, but you've got to take what's left. You've got to survive and tell our story." I couldn't listen anymore, and I wouldn't take the money either. The thought of his money belt around my waist was unbearable.

"I can't take it, Anthony. I've got this crazy thing about money. It'll bring me nothing but trouble. Look, I've been threatened with blackmail too. But I can't pay, so I just deny it and dare them to prove it. Having the money to pay would only convince them they're right. And if they find it on me, I'm finished."

Anthony seemed to be listening. Perhaps I convinced him. I got up to go, but as I left he tried to slip a diamond ring and some earrings into my pocket. I protested. "Weren't you listening?"

"Once they kill me, you'll be on your own. Keep this stuff, it's not money, and you never know when you'll need something. Please." He pushed me out the door. "Go now . . . and God be with you."

As I trudged away, snowflakes melted on my warm face, mingling with my tears. Things just never got any better.

Another night passed and I was back at work. Standing behind the counter, I reflected that I had only been in the "new world" for two months, yet it felt like forever. Anthony's impending doom overwhelmed me. I had to see him once more. I decided to slip out during lunch.

I rushed through the streets in my brown shop uniform, ran up the three flights to his place, and rang the bell. The landlady answered the door. Her face looked sickly and pale as she led me into the living room and sat me down.

"Last night, an hour after you left, Mr. Anthony had a visitor. After a while there was a gun shot. And then the visitor came out. He told me he had to kill the Jew because there was nothing more to be had from him. He said he'd send the German police to take away the body. They'll be here shortly. Can you wait and answer a couple of questions for them?"

She left me alone in the room, and I heard a van pull up to the house. I had to get out, fast. I went into the kitchen and down the fire stairs. Once out the back door I went around to the front, and from the alley I saw them carrying down Anthony's body.

Just then a streetcar clattered to a stop. I crossed to it and hopped on. I would let it take me wherever it was going.

What was I to do now? The Gestapo was bound to start looking for me at work and at my room. If the thugs had told the Gestapo about the killing, they must have mentioned me as well. I couldn't even risk going back to my room. But I had nothing, not even a coat. I was wearing a thin suit under a brown uniform smock. The first thing to do was to get rid of the smock. I pushed it under my seat. I looked in my purse—not enough money on me for a ticket to Lwów, to Mati and Edward.

Suddenly I noticed the little diamond ring on my finger, Anthony's parting gift. And then there were the earrings in my purse. It was sure to be dangerous, but maybe I could sell them. The next problem was to whom. I didn't know anyone who was buying. Then the Ukrainian liaison lawyer came to mind. It was a risk. I might end up with nothing. He could even turn me over to the Germans. But there was no alternative.

I found my man at home and decided to tell him the whole truth for a change. He was furious. "The gall, claiming to be a Ukrainian patriot. Why, I ought to pitch you down the stairs, Jewess."

But then he looked at the ring. I had asked only fifty zlotys. He tossed the money at me and grabbed the ring as I pulled it off. Without another word he hustled me out the door.

The next train to Lwów was four hours away. I sent Edward a wire and started circling the streets around the station to kill time. The streets were safer than the waiting rooms haunted by police and thugs searching for Jews. As I walked along I noticed a new poster. It was a warning to the Gentile population to be on the lookout for Jews on false identity papers. Those helping Jews were subject to execution. But now there was a one-hundred-zloty bounty on each Jew turned in to the authorities. This was sure to increase business for the Szmalcownicy. Now they'd be able to shake us down and then, when they'd picked us clean, turn us over to the "master race" at twice the old price. I was glad to be leaving Warsaw. Whatever else awaited me in Lwów, Mati would be there.

The time passed quickly, and soon enough I was on the train. I had no luggage, just my papers showing me to be a pure Aryan.

As the train picked up speed, I forced myself to think of Lwów and my friends. I could not afford to think of Anthony.

10

Back to Lwów

It was early in the morning when my train pulled into Lwów. I felt a certain amount of assurance as, this time, I knew the town. And then I saw Edward waiting for me at the end of the platform. I rushed into his arms, blinded by uncontrollable tears of happiness.

He held me close. "Hush. No time for tears." And with that he took my arm and led me out of the station. We climbed on a tram for Mati's place on Halicka Street. I had not seen her since the darkest times of the Kolomyja ghetto. Before we went into the apartment, Edward stopped to brief me on the setup. There would be the landlady to deal with and I had to learn the script.

Mati was now billed as the daughter of a landowner who came to town occasionally to replenish his daughter's wardrobe. Edward was her fiancé. I was to be a university student down from Warsaw for a short holiday. Some distance from the reality of death and destruction we had just left in Kolomyja.

After smiling our way through the introductions, we closed the door. Mati and I collapsed into each other's arms. Edward stood aside and gave us our moment of closeness. But then he urged us to keep our emotions and our voices under control. "It's too easy for the landlady to hear us. She'll be suspicious anyway."

We let go of each other, sat down, and began to tell our stories. First Mati, with a horror tale not unlike my own.

She had arrived in Lwów just two days after I had left. She had come in with a Christian friend, a girl from a small town near Kolomyja. They'd separated at the railway station, and Mati went to look for me at the address I'd given her. How could she know she was walking into the trap set by my own hasty departure?

"Your friend left several days ago, along with a fellow visiting her. They were running for their lives. Jews on false papers."

Mati withdrew hastily and headed back to the center of town. She knew it well, having studied at the university before the war. She decided to try the place her friend had gone and tell her she would go back to the Kolomyja ghetto, where her family remained. It was foolishness, she concluded, to try to escape, and now she was angry that she had given in to Nunek's pleas that she get out. He had hoped that she could bring the rest of the family later.

When Mati got to her traveling companion's address, she found a party in full swing. She was welcomed and made part of the merriment. Just as she began to relax, a young man cornered her.

"So you're Mrs. Najder," he whispered, "the pharmacist's wife from Kolomyja? Olga says you're a graduate of the university here in Lwów. Polish literature, right?" He did not pause for answers to these questions. "Say, that was a nice fur jacket you came in with. You know that Jews aren't permitted to own fur anymore."

Mati turned away as discreetly as possible, made for the door, and slipped out into the street.

But as she looked back, the young man was following. She walked faster and then cut into the courtyard of an apartment house. She thought she had lost him but decided to stand in the shadows until dark. It was evening when she finally ventured out into the street again. But there he was, standing on the other side of the street, waiting. He crossed to her.

"You won't run away again, will you? What do you say we go dancing? Over to Gestapo headquarters."

Mati pulled free and began to run. She knew the town well and took full advantage of its crooked little streets, ducking in and out of back alleys and arcades for two hours till she was certain she'd shaken him.

Unable to go anywhere else, she remembered the address I'd given her on Halicka Street. Even though she'd never laid eyes on Edward before, she decided to go and introduce herself as a friend of "Mr. Stanislau Glac" (Edward's alias). Perhaps they'd have a room for her.

The name worked like an engraved invitation. No questions were asked, and within a moment she was offered a room. After a night's sleep, Mati went out to wander around the town she'd known so well. Suddenly her path was blocked by a militiaman, a Ukrainian.

"Halt. You're under arrest, Jewess."

First she protested, but when this had no effect, she began to implore, then to beg. Nothing worked. She was being dragged closer and closer to Gestapo headquarters when she finally dug in her heels and stopped.

"What are you doing this for? There's nothing for you turning me in. Let me go and I'll give you all my money and jewelry, OK?"

His hold loosened. "Now you're talking. Let's see if it's worth doing business." He changed course and took Mati to a deserted part of town. Mati had to strip to her underwear while the militiaman went through her garments inch by inch, cutting open the linings to make sure she wasn't getting away with a thing. He took her money, her watch and wedding ring, a small gold chain, everything. Then he shredded her identity papers, the birth certificate, and domicile police registration—things worth far more than the paltry sum she had given him.

In tears, Mati asked that he leave her enough for a ticket home. After some thought, he handed her a few zlotys and let her go.

Shaken, she walked out of the room determined to go straight back to the Kolomyja ghetto. At the station, she discovered that there was no train for Kolomyja until the next morning. There was nothing to do but go back to Halicka Street for another night. There she learned that a visitor had come for her and said he would come again: "Mr. Stanislau Glac." But the name meant nothing to Mati, as she'd never met him and cared nothing for what he might have to say. All she wanted to do was get back to her husband, her parents, her sisters and nephews, and their two cramped rooms in the Kolomyja ghetto. Why had she let Nunek talk her into trying to escape? It was useless. Lost in her thoughts, she did not hear the knock at her door.

Edward, the friend she had never met, entered quickly, smiling broadly. With the landlady hovering over his shoulder, he made a vast show of warm greeting, expressing great joy at seeing her again after so long. Satisfied at the meeting of old acquaintances, the landlady retreated to the kitchen. Mati closed the door, and Edward introduced himself.

"Well, how have you managed so far?" Ten minutes later Edward had heard the whole story. "I want to help you all I can. You're Blanca's friend and that's all I need to know."

Mati could only smile weakly. "Thanks, but all I want is to get back to Kolomyja."

"That's suicide. Once you've made the break you've got to go the whole way. You can't go back. And you still have a chance to save the rest of your family."

They argued back and forth, but Edward finally won her over. "I'll start out seeing you regularly. Later we can call it an engagement. That'll keep the landlady satisfied."

Edward went out of the room for a moment. "I've squared it with the landlady. I told her you'd only be here a couple of days, so she needn't bother about police registration."

Within a few days, through a Gentile pharmacist in Kolomyja, Mati was able to reach her husband and get a new set of identity papers. Then she registered at the police prefect's office as Kazimiera Kowalska. "That's my story." Tears filled her eyes and she reached for me again. "It doesn't matter. Just so long as you're here with me. Together we'll face the world. Maybe we'll survive." She looked at me. "Now, tell me what's happened to you. It seems so long ago since you left the ghetto in Kolomyja. Remember how you left? We were in that tiny little room, and I was so jealous of your courage."

By the time I had recounted my own trials in the Aryan world, it was late. Edward left us for the night, and we settled down to sleep.

Neither Mati nor I dared to go out much. Her papers weren't legal yet and I was too scared to set foot in the city. Since I was visiting on university holidays, the landlady made no demand that I register. But I couldn't just sit around forever. I was a visitor and had to be interested in the sights and sounds of the city. So we began to venture out, walking along the busy streets, mainly window shopping. Edward came every day. And his air of nobility, humor, and warmth made us feel comfortable beyond measure. He looked the part of Polish aristocracy, luxuriant whiskers and mustache, gay exuberance, all fitting the important position he held in the German administration. He lived his new life as though he had been born to authority and dependability. Regular in his church attendance, he had a wide circle of Polish and German friends.

As the end of my "visit" to Lwów approached, Mati invented a new story for her landlady. She was going to take me home to visit her family. Would our room be available when we returned? Everything was arranged, and one morning we packed for our visit and left. We went no further, however, than the other side of town, where Edward had rented another room for us. A week later we reappeared at Mrs. Malinowska's and took up residence again on Halicka Street. It was there we felt safest. But a few days later she looked in on us.

"I'm sorry to trouble you, but you really must register with the prefect's office. There are just too many strangers in town, and besides the caretaker's son says he saw you around town the day before you came back, and he's asking questions. He thinks I'm keeping illegal lodgers. In fact, he said he thinks you're Jews."

"Absurd!" we laughed. Nevertheless, it was time to move on, despite the dangers of looking for another place. We spent a couple of days following leads in the classified advertisements of the newspaper, but the rooms were always rented by the time we got there. One evening, we decided to be up at 5:00 A.M. to get the paper when it arrived at the kiosk around the corner.

At 4:00 that morning I awoke. Restless and unable to sleep, I dressed and slipped out of the building. I was chilled by the empty streets and greyness of the morning. By the time I got to the kiosk, the newspapers had already arrived. I bought a couple and headed back.

I was about to turn into Halicka Street, when I heard my name called out, "Blanca." My real name, not the one on my Aryan papers. Panic-stricken, I rushed on. Again it came louder and imploringly, "Blanca, wait . . . please." This time it stopped me in my tracks. I turned to see someone running toward me, pulling a small boy along behind her. Behind her followed another figure. It was Frania, Mati's older sister, with her three-year-old son, Leszek, and her sister-in-law Helen. As they reached me I could read their story on their faces. The Kolomyja ghetto had been destroyed, and they'd escaped its last gasp. It was February 2, 1943.

Without a word, I led them up to the apartment and into our room. Frania and Helen looked dreadful. Unwashed, their clothes were streaked with mud and dust, their eyes full of horror, while their mouths were wreathed in pitiful smiles of relief. Even before we were able to make them comfortable, Frania began.

"Kolomyja is Judenrein. The last Action was finished yesterday. They started to kill everybody. We managed to get over the wall. There's no one left. They killed everybody . . ." Frania's voice fell away, but she kept repeating these last words.

Helen was in worse shape. She was pulling at her hair and had stuffed a handkerchief in her mouth to muffle her cries. Through it we could still make out her words. "My God, what have I done, I'll never rest . . . I've killed my baby."

"What do you mean?"

"I left him. I just left him in his crib for a German bullet. Just got over the wall and ran."

There was nothing to say. We could only try to calm her. We had to start planning for how to deal with this new problem right away. But instead, Mati kept asking questions. She wanted details. How did her parents die? What of her husband, Nunek, her fifteen-year-old nephew, Menek, and her older sister Cyla?

"All dead. Except maybe Menek," Frania answered. It appeared to her that Menek, who was driven out of the ghetto with the family, was able to slip away and keep running. A guard shot at him. But he just might have made it.

Frania continued: "The rest of the family was taken away in the middle of the night and dragged barefoot on icy streets, chased by vicious dogs toward Szeparowce Forest. We could hear the shots coming from that direction."

"How'd you get to Lwów?"

"After we got over the wall, we walked to the next town down the rail line and found a train. We got in late last night, but we were too scared to check in at any hotel. One look at us and they'd guess. Once during the night we spotted a light in one of the buildings and, hoping that this was a hotel where we could get a room for a few hours' sleep, we turned there. When we got closer, we realized that we were about to walk into Gestapo headquarters. We kept walking. We didn't have your address. Nunek was the only one who did. So we just walked all night, resting on the park benches."

"It's a miracle no one picked you up."

"And another one when we spotted Blanca on the street."

As we sat staring at each other through the mist of tears, Leszek began to whimper and then cry. We heard Mrs. Malinowska in the kitchen starting to get breakfast ready. She'd find out about our guests sooner or later. I decided that it might as well be now.

I laughed out loud, asked our guests if they'd like some tea, and came out of our room headed for the kitchen.

"Good morning, Mrs. Malinowska. You'll never guess what happened. I was going out to get a paper when I ran into some old friends who've just come into town." I watched her. The weak smile showed she couldn't quite believe the coincidence, but she wanted to be sympathetic. Perhaps it was her soft spot for Mr. Glac, his friends, and their friends too. I poured the boiling water into some cups, found a tray, and returned to the room. Leszek was already curled up asleep on the couch. The sisters were sitting close together, while Helen had moved to a shadowy corner of the room.

It was clear that they couldn't stay with us. But the women had managed to get away with some money and jewelry. More important, they had an address, a contact in Lwów. It was the cousin of a dentist in Kolomyja, a man who was in contact with people who produced forged identity cards and birth certificates. He himself was living on false papers, but he had known Frania and Mati's family well. He'd be sure to help.

This contact turned out to be a lucky break for all of us. First, he got Frania and Helen some papers. Then he found Frania, Helen, and the child a room with a family to whom the truth could be told. The family was willing to take on these dangerous boarders, but only on condition that they not go out at all. All their needs would be seen to, but only if they stayed inside. After all, the little boy was a dead giveaway and could get them all in trouble. Confinement was going to be hard on him, but there was no alternative.

Mati and I were permitted to visit, and we became eyes and ears for the shut-ins. Soon thereafter we managed to find a new place ourselves, a room on Wolna Street, close to the town citadel. This time we used some of Frania's money to acquire phony police registrations. We wanted no more inquiries and accusations. Frania's contact got them for us. After the trouble it had taken to find new lodgings, we couldn't afford to lose them.

Each day the papers reported more and more arrests of Jews. But this time it was distinguished people, those who had thought themselves safe by reason of marriage or conversion, or even Poles with a Jewish parent or grandparent. The Reich laws were catching up with everyone. And besides the parasites—the Szmalcownicy—were as busy as in Warsaw, doing a flourishing trade in extortion and blackmail. The worst of it was the glee with which patriotic Poles greeted each new denunciation. To them, the German occupation wasn't unmitigated evil. At least they were getting rid of the Jews, "our misfortune."

In spite of all this, we went on fighting. One day, clutching our false papers, we walked into the employment office, trying to act like any other pair of unemployed Poles looking for work. As in Warsaw, there was work to be had—with the Germans. Women were needed at the German military hospital. Mati was taken on in the pharmacy, quite by chance, for it would have been dangerous to have admitted knowing as much about drugs as she had learned from her husband. I became a maid on one of the wards.

The German military had taken over this hospital and now it was full of soldiers wounded in the fighting in the Soviet Union. The wards were filled with frostbite cases, and there was a shortage of physicians and trained nurses. But the pharmacy was well stocked and the kitchens full of food. Patient morale was low, and the talk among the men was more about home and family than glory and conquest.

Since Mati and I were just "Polish trash," uneducated laborers, no one supposed we could understand more than rudimentary German. But as I carried bedpans back and forth, I'd linger to catch a word or two about the front. The talk was often about the Reds' murderous tanks and their rockets, the Katiushas, that rained devastation across the battle lines. New arrivals kept bringing bad news. Then the newspapers began to report planned retreats, shortenings of the front, and withdrawals.

At the end of January 1943, we had read about the defeat at Voronez. Now we heard reports of evacuations from Rostov. Even reports of victories were revealing; in the middle of March the big news was of the great recapture of Charkov. By the end of the month, the hospital was filled with new casualties and reports of heavy German losses.

In addition to helping nurses, I was assigned to floor and staircase scrubbing. It was a backbreaking task that exhausted me daily. Mati was more fortunate. She was proving herself invaluable in the pharmacy and became the supervisor's favorite. Of course she knew far more about the work than she could let on. Neither of us earned much, but the food was good and, unlike anywhere else in town, there was enough of it. We began to feel fairly secure in this German bastion and got on with the unsuspecting Herrenvolk. It was the Poles we had to worry about. They had a nose for little things the Germans would never see, and it was impossible to hide every subtle difference of background, for we didn't even know what all of them were. Even a trivial thing like eyeglasses could have given me away. I had to stop wearing them, despite my nearsightedness. It was better to squint and stare, to stick my nose into my work, than to look different, to be seen as any-

thing other than a poor peasant girl. Glasses could earn you the mock-
ery of "intellectual," which might soon become "Bolshie," or even
"Jew."

One day, Mati was complimented for her work by the German
pharmacist who supervised her. "You really seem too intelligent for
this sort of routine job." More than once a German doctor had said
the same thing to me. These were danger signals. They meant we
weren't playing our parts well enough. In general, we had to feign ignorance of much that we understood, especially the German used by
the administrators. Our only concession to ourselves was the practice
of meeting a couple of times a day. We'd have our lunches and sup-
pers together, just to touch base. But this meant going several floors
out of my way, and it began to arouse suspicion among the Polish
workers. So we had to cut these meetings down.

Our lives began to take on the texture of routine. Jobs, food, and
friendship relaxed us a great deal. We did our work. We tried to come
and go unobtrusively. Sometimes we'd manage to smuggle out a bit of
food for Mati's family. It was a special pleasure to see Leszek's joy at
receiving an orange or a candy treat. We didn't visit as often as we
wished, for we didn't want to annoy the family boarding them.

In our new place, we too had to be cautious. Our landlords had
decided to claim the status of "Volksdeutsche," mainly for the larger
rations and other benefits involved. They were full of enthusiasm for
the new order and eager to pass along reports of new Actions in the
ghetto. One evening, the lady of the house shared a secret with us.

"You know, there are lots of Jews who've gotten out of the ghetto
and are using forged documents to live on the outside. I never told you,
but the very room you two are in was rented by a couple of Jewesses
with phony papers. The Gestapo took them away not two weeks before you got here. You never can tell."

We nodded and tisked in agreement, then slowly rose and withdrew
to our room.

Soon thereafter we had a fright. The adjoining room was about to
be let to a couple of Ukrainians from, of all places, Kolomyja. We began to plan for the worst, but in the end they didn't find the room suitable and left after a couple of days.

We learned to feign disinterest as our landlady gossiped around the
kitchen table. When required to respond to her stories we used our
imaginations, glibly fabricating as required. Alone we'd often reflect

on why our compatriots had sold out so cheaply to the occupiers. We'd recall the old Polish song that everyone had sung before the war, with the refrain, "We'll never let the Germans spit in our faces, nor let them Teutonize our children." What had made them such willing lackeys?

Sometimes I compared our lot to that of prisoners under long sentences. The difference was that we had no idea how long our sentences were, nor when they would be changed to death. For Mati, it must have been harder to "serve time" in Lwów. She still had friends in the town from her university days, some of whom she remembered as humane and committed antifascists. But when she approached them now, she was met by fear and by resentment at our imposition. There was one old friend who'd been a link at first between Mati and her husband, routing messages to another Gentile friend in Kolomyja. But after he learned of the final razing of the Kolomyja ghetto, he didn't bother to hide his relief.

"So, now that your family's gone, you won't need my help anymore, right?"

We consoled ourselves by thinking how enormous the risk was for anyone who did help. And yet some did.

Nothing good could last very long. One morning just as we were about to leave for work, the doorbell rang. It was Frania, with Leszek and Helen in tow. Once in our room, they told us they'd been forced to leave their room, but not before the family they'd paid so much to had sold them out to the extortionists. The previous night they'd had "guests," who'd taken all the money and jewels left. This morning they'd been turned out, with nothing left but what they had hidden with us. Evidently, the chance of a quick killing had been too much for their hosts to pass up.

We didn't go to work that day at all. We had to find shelter for the family right away. It was agreed that I'd take Leszek to some people Frania knew, Jews living on forged papers outside of Lwów. We'd meet later in the day at a bookshop where a friend of Mati's worked.

Things went well enough until after the rendezvous at the bookshop. We were on our way out with the address of a safe place to stay when Mati noticed an old acquaintance from her university days. The woman ignored Mati's quiet greeting, and we hurried out the door.

We headed for a nearby cafe, took a table, and ordered coffee. We needed to take stock and plan our next step. As we made ourselves comfortable, a policeman entered the shop, looked around, and took a seat at the table next to ours. Mati's chair faced the cafe window, and through it she could see the form of her fellow student, the woman she'd noticed when leaving the bookstore. Evidently, she had given us away to the policeman.

We obviously had to split up to shake the policeman off our trail. We agreed to meet at a millinery shop we knew on Halicka Street as soon as we could. Frania and Helen got up, took their leave, and went off in opposite directions. Mati and I stayed on a few minutes more, sipping our coffees as the policeman looked on. When we rose and paid the bill, the policeman did likewise and followed us into the street. After twenty minutes of doubling back and forth in the crowds on the city's principal avenues, we were sure we'd shaken him. We made our way to the millinery shop where we found the others trying on hats. With a sigh of relief we joined them.

Two minutes later, the shop door opened and the policeman came in. With a peremptory gesture, he ordered us out of the shop and told us to follow him. On the street he announced: "I've a witness you're all Jewesses. You'll all have to come along to Gestapo headquarters."

There seemed nothing to do but follow his order. As we walked along, we began again to bargain for our lives, and as before, it worked. We all turned into a courtyard, where he quickly relieved us of what money and jewels we had left and let us go.

The incident left me wondering what that educated young woman thought she was doing. Did her deed leave her with the satisfied feelings of a patriot, freeing Poland of four more Jewish women?

We went back to Halicka Street, where we managed to place Frania and Helen in our old room with Mrs. Malinowska, the old lady who couldn't be bothered with "politics" and let her rooms to anyone who could pay. The next day, Mati and I returned to work.

There were no questions about our missed day, and in fact the next few weeks passed uneventfully. Frania and Helen found new rooms, and since the people who rented to them didn't know their true identities, the two women were able to come and go freely.

Spring 1943 came, and April wakened us to feelings of optimism. Perhaps we'd survive to see Hitler's final defeat. If we could be sure that the defeat would happen, death would be a little easier to take, or so we thought until death once again stared us fully in the face.

One day I was called suddenly from stair scrubbing to the main office. The first person I saw on entering was Mati, white-faced.

"What's happened?" I whispered.

"We're finished, that's what."

We were denounced again by Mati's fellow student, the woman who tried to sell us out earlier to the Ukrainian policeman in the street. She must have followed us to our workplace and informed Mati's supervisor that he harbored a Jew.

As the supervisor picked up the phone to call the hospital guard, Mati got out through the window and beckoned me to follow her. We started to run. Looking over our shoulders as we ran, we noticed a Gestapo car parked in front of the pharmacy. Obviously, they had already been informed and were ready to pick us up.

We managed to get home just for a few minutes. We quickly threw together a couple of essentials for survival, especially money and our identity papers. We told the landlady that Mati's father had just died and we had been called away to the funeral. "We will be back in a couple of days," we assured her.

Fifteen minutes later, we were in Mrs. Malinowska's place on Halicka Street. Safe for the moment. Somehow we got word to Edward and asked him to find out what happened after our escape. He promised to use his contacts and told us to sit tight. He'd be with us as soon as he could.

That evening he came for us. "Your situation is pretty awful. The Gestapo is after you all right. They searched your rooms and now they've got a search on, pictures of both of you on the notice board with the other wanted posters, and a warning to arrest on sight or notify the police if you're seen. How did they ever get the pictures?"

"We had to submit them for the jobs at the hospital."

"I see. Well, let's see how we can get you out of Lwów. It won't be easy. Everyone in the hospital knows what you look like, and besides, there's a one-thousand-zloty bounty on your heads."

We had to keep off the streets, but we couldn't stay on Halicka Street either. It would put the other two women at risk, as well as the old lady who had helped us so many times. So that night, we slipped out and Edward brought us to the home of some friends. They were a Catholic man and his wife, a convert from Judaism. The couple was hiding a young Jewish orphan. They greeted us warmly, but it was clear that we couldn't find refuge with them for long. So we sat down at the kitchen table and plotted our escape from Lwów.

The only way was by an evening train for Warsaw, and that would mean passing through an identity check at the station. Edward got hold of the tickets, and we attempted to develop some disguises from the peasant clothes that he was able to rustle up. With everyone's help, we soon seemed unrecognizable.

With some money from Edward and Frania, we slipped out of the apartment, heading for the station and the 1:30 A.M. train. The first thing we noticed at the station was our pictures among the police-wanted posters.

Mati walked away from me and headed for the line at the platform barrier. It would be safer to pass through separately. Once she got through, I marched resolutely forward and thrust my papers at the gatekeeper. Just then, the train whistle sounded, and without further scrutiny he waved me through. I caught up to Mati further down the platform, and we hopped aboard the nearest car.

The train was dark because of the blackout rules, so we held each other's hands tightly as we pushed through the corridors filled with travelers. In the end, we found two seats on the wooded slats of a third-class carriage. With a sudden lurch, the train began to move out of the station, and we began to think we might make it after all. As we sat there, feeling the train gather steam, I thought I heard the word *Jews*. Cocking my ear, I caught one traveler speaking to another somewhere in the darkness.

"You hear about the ghetto in Warsaw? The Jews have got guns, they're fighting the Germans street by street."

The glory of this news blotted all other thoughts from my mind. To fight, to die with honor. Was it true? We needed to know every detail, yet we couldn't show the slightest interest. So we just listened, gleaning scraps and snatches of the talk around us.

"Where'd they get the guns?"

"Leave it to the Jews, those bastards can get hold of anything." A third voice interjected: "No it's the underground who's passing them the stuff. I heard that in Warsaw a couple of days ago."

"Just like those socialist traitors," the first voice responded. "They'll stoop to anything."

Active resistance in the Warsaw ghetto? We did not dare believe it. If the news were true, we thought, our lives and struggles would take on a different meaning. To fight, to resist, to avenge ourselves and our martyred dear ones was all that mattered.

Lost in these thoughts through the long night, we could finally feel

the train slowing down as it began to enter the station. WARSZAWA—
the sign slipped by as the train came finally to a full stop. We disem-
barked and began walking down the platform toward the exit.

We had reached our destination with some hope and, now, renewed
anticipation. Little did we know then that Warsaw held a very different future for us.

11

Warsaw Again

It was early on Good Friday morning in April 1943 when the train pulled in. Warsaw station seemed unusually full of police, on the platform, in the waiting rooms, everywhere. Taking no notice of them, we let the surging crowds carry us out of the station and onto one of Warsaw's loveliest boulevards, the Aleje Jerozolimskie. But before we had moved a hundred yards from the station, our path was blocked by two men in civilian clothes. Wordlessly they handed us over to a couple of uniformed policemen. Still without a word of explanation they began firmly to herd us in the direction of the police station across the square. They ignored our protests and questions. They did not even turn their heads to look at us as we walked along.

"It must be my Semitic looks," Mati whispered under her breath.

I turned to her with annoyance. "We admit nothing, right?" She nodded agreement. Now that Jews were fighting, we would struggle too. The thrill of danger strengthened our wills to survive.

Still without explanation, a precinct warden led us to a small room and locked us in. We had vital decisions to make and little time. We had the addresses of a couple of Jews living on false papers in Warsaw, parting gifts from Edward and our last refuge in Lwów. These people were to put us in touch with the Polish underground. The first thing to do was to tear up the paper containing this information and swallow it. Relieved that we were sparing these people from further risk, we awaited interrogation more calmly.

Soon enough it began. The interrogator wore the uniform of the

Polish State Police. He began kindly enough. But he soon lost patience with our stubborn denials.

"You're both Jewesses. That's plain enough."

"No, it's not so!"

"Where are you from?"

"Lwów."

"Why'd you come to Warsaw?"

"Furlough, to enjoy the Easter holidays."

"Lies," he exclaimed. "You're escaping from the ghetto. Like rats leaving a sinking ship. We're picking your sort up everywhere."

"We don't have anything to do with those people. We don't know anything about it."

And so it went, assertion and denial, for over two hours. We managed to show increasing indignation over these "baseless" charges. "Shame on you, that you should destroy your Polish brethren's Good Friday like this. All we came here for was to celebrate the resurrection of our savior."

My speech was interrupted by a peel of sarcastic laughter. "Who are you visiting in town? Where are you staying?"

"We don't know anyone here. We were going to check into a hotel and see the sights. But if we'd known what dangers the capital holds for Christian women, we'd have gone somewhere else. Who would have expected such abuse, and at the hands of our countryman?"

All this complaint produced was increased irritation.

"At Gestapo headquarters you'd be singing a different tune. They'd turn you into soap."

"Well, if good Polish Christians are being turned into soap by the Germans, we might as well all give up in shame!"

In a fury, the interrogator began to shout. "Stop playing the innocents, you bitches." Pointing at Mati, he continued: "I'd mark you a Jewess in any crowd." Then he turned to me. "Look, blondie, maybe you're a Gentile, but you'll catch it for hiding this Jew-bitch. You know the law. It's death for protecting them. Look, I'll give you a couple of minutes to yourselves. When I come back I want the truth." He stomped from the cell, slamming the door behind him.

Though exhausted, we still felt confident in our decision to fight, even if the Gestapo were brought in. As long as we continued to deny the charge, nothing could be done to prove it.

"But what about torture?" Mati wondered.

"Let them kill us! No more easy victories!"

Half an hour later, the door opened, and another officer handed us a typed statement to sign.

"We have no proof that you're Jews, so just sign this and you can go."

It was too neat not to be a trick of some sort. "What's this paper all about?"

"Just a formality," he answered blandly.

"Well, we won't sign anything unless we can read the entire statement. Then we'll sign. OK?"

The policeman tossed the paper at us. "It's just a silly formality."

But as we read it we began to laugh. "Yes, it's nothing, nothing but an admission that we are guilty of what you've accused us of." Mati pushed the papers back at the man. "How can you ask as to sign lies like this? How can we admit to being what we aren't?"

"All right, you two are just too smart for your own good. We'll just have to send you elsewhere."

"Where to?"

"Gestapo headquarters."

"Fine," we retorted, "maybe the Germans will get it straight when our Polish brothers can't!"

The policeman turned and left, but the cell door remained open. In came a man in plainclothes, a detective evidently, who led us into an office nearby.

"So, ladies. Please give me your addresses in Lwów and your places of employment."

There was nothing for it but to tell the truth, and without hesitation.

"Thank you. Now, if you have no objections, I'll just make some calls to check these details."

"Not at all, go right ahead." I responded with a confidence sinking into despair. Now we knew the game was finished. The German hospital in Lwów would seal our fates. The detective picked up the phone to call the local Gestapo headquarters. He was clearly dissatisfied with the conversation. Long-distance calls on nonmilitary matters were not allowed. The problem would have to be dealt with locally. "But it's hard to tell with women." He nodded his head. "Yes, I understand, but they insist they're Gentiles." Then he shook his head. "No, we're not through yet. We still have some further steps to see if they're telling the truth." He hung up and turned to us. "Back to solitary ladies."

By now it was well past noon, and again the cell door opened, revealing our previous interrogator and a new face, one of the men who had picked us up outside the train station. This plainclothesman turned out to be a Ukrainian. The interrogator and he exchanged a few words, and then the uniformed policeman went out. A moment later he was back, with a priest. Evidently, we were about to be led through the catechism.

Mati and I smiled secretly to each other. Years in the Polish school system had fully prepared us for this little quiz. We went through the rituals and the prayers simply and flawlessly. But perhaps we were too good. For the priest turned to the interrogator and frowned.

"These two have learned their catechism too well!" With that he left.

The others began again. "Now, give us the address of someone in Warsaw who will vouch for you. Someone who knew you before the war. Then we'll let you go."

"But I told you, we're from Lwów. We don't know anyone here. Look, just call our families or our employer in Lwów." It was easy to suggest the impossible.

The uniformed policeman looked at me and motioned to the door. "You, come with me." He took me to an adjoining cell and sat me down. "Look, we know you're not Jewish. But why cover for her? Save your skin. Tell us the truth and we'll let you go."

"But I can't lie. She's a good Christian girl like me from a good Christian family as far back as you can go."

With a shrug, he brought me back into Mati's cell, and we were locked in for the rest of the day. At nightfall they began to demand our signatures on the "formality" once again. We continued to refuse.

"Sir, we've been here all day. Could we have something to drink?"

Soon thereafter, coffee and sandwiches arrived. We were too scared to be hungry, but we made a show of eating ravenously.

And now a new ploy was tried. I was to be released unconditionally, but Mati was to remain.

"I won't leave without her. You have no reason to keep her."

Mati began to whisper: "Get out. Take the money. Head for Krakow. Just tell Frania what happened to me."

"Hush up. We'll both survive or die together." She subsided, and we prepared to wait out the night. But a bit later a new officer came in, removed Mati, and locked the door again. An hour later he was back, with Mati still in tow.

"My name is Stach," said the policeman. "You two are free to go."
We suspected another ruse, but the officer ushered us out of the cell,
through the office, and into the street. We really were free after all.

As we walked out into the dark and empty streets, I could hardly
contain myself. "Out with it. What happened?"

Mati began an incredible tale. "Well, Stach took me out of the cell
and led me into the street. We walked along till we got to a bar he
seemed to know. It was on Aleje Jerozolimskie, and then he told me to
wait while he went in. I must have stood there an hour. After the first
couple of minutes with no one around, I guess I could have run off and
tried to lose myself in the crowd. But they still had you, and besides,
what if it was just another police trick? If I ran, they'd know they were
right after all. So I did what I was told. I just stood there. All of a sudden the policeman came out. The first thing he said was, 'All right,
now you've convinced me. If you'd been Jewish, you would have run.
But you stayed put. Let's go back to the lockup. You and your friend
will be free to go.' That's it."

I listened to Mati's story in disbelief, relief, and gratitude. But by the
time she finished, I had started looking around cautiously. Sure
enough, there behind us in the darkness was Stach, not just stalking
us but catching up. Before I could even warn Mati our reprieve was
over, he'd caught up.

"You're probably wondering where to stay tonight. Permit me to
help. I know a nice place in a private home where no questions will be
asked."

We were too thunderstruck to speak. But somehow we felt Stach
was a friend. We'd take a chance. Our hunch was right, as we had
many occasions to reflect thereafter. Though he never admitted it, we
came to believe that Officer Stach had underground connections and
had been planted at the police station.

The room he found for us was as described, and after a night's rest
we ventured out into the streets. The ghetto, we learned, was still
fighting; Jews were taking Germans with them to their graves, but the
battle was nearly over, and it was too late for us to sacrifice our lives.
As we walked along we could see the trucks pass, coming back from
the ghetto loaded with wounded Germans. The spectacle seemed holy
to us.

A week later the ghetto was still unconquered. How long could it
hold out? We tried desperately to find someone who could tell us how

things stood. There seemed no way in; all the entrances had been sealed. There was nothing to do but legalize our position in Warsaw. This would mean, once more, police registrations and jobs. We knew that we might still be under suspicion, so we did not use the addresses we had gotten in Lwów.

My first stop was the general government internal passport office. During my last stay in Warsaw, before going back to Lwów, I had applied for an ID card, a "Kennkarte." I had left some perfectly genuine documents at the passport office, including a valid birth certificate under the name I'd first come to Warsaw with, Bronislava Panasiak. In hopes that the application had been processed and was still waiting for me, I presented myself there. It was entirely possible, of course, that my true identity had been discovered and that the Gestapo lay in wait for me. But I managed to walk right into the lion's den and out again, successfully. All I had to do was sign for the card, a document validated by the German general government until 1948! I was now as legal as anyone could be.

Mati's position was not so firm. All she had were her rather doubtful false papers, and these could not withstand the scrutiny required for a Kennkarte. Since my original application six months before, the investigation had become far more thorough. What she needed was a new set, including a birth certificate, that would withstand real inquiries. So we approached our policeman, Stach, who was only too glad to provide a contact.

"You can trust this guy," said Stach. "He'll get you a whole set of documents, including a filled-out Kennkarte, for a nominal fee."

The fee was hardly nominal, but soon enough Mati had a new identity: Maria Bielska. She liked her new first name, and she has been Maria ever since.

Now that we had documentation, we began looking for a place to live. For safety we decided to rent rooms in different places. Almost immediately I found a room with a widow on Aleje Niepodleglosci—Independence Avenue. And just as quickly, the building caretaker asked for my papers for police registration. He examined them closely and then looked up at my face. I couldn't tell what he read in it, but as he handed the documents back to me, he said: "Good enough, but see that you don't bring any suspicious visitors around."

Finding a place for Maria was not so simple. Without my blond hair and blue eyes, she looked suspicious and met with several refusals.

"I'm sorry. Your papers look all right, but we can't afford to take any risks these days," said the more honest landladies. In the end, the best Maria could do was rent a bed in a house of doubtful repute near the ghetto. She spent several nights there in the company of prostitutes and street people. Although they proved kind and considerate, I was terrified for her.

One day, Maria turned up at my room looking really frightened. That morning as she left her place, a gaggle of children, some no more than ten or eleven years old, began to follow her, shrieking, "Look, a Jewess out of the ghetto. Hey, where's your arm band, lady?"

A crowd gathered. Maria decided to take action before suspicion was aroused. She turned on the urchins, grabbed one by the arm, and began dragging him along.

"Where you taking me?"

"To the police, to lodge a complaint for harassment," Maria replied. This set the younger ones to flight. The older ones suggested a fifty-zloty bribe as the price for leaving her undisturbed. At this Maria turned to the bystanders. "Has anyone seen a policeman? These thugs have got to be put away." At this, the teenagers decided it was time to disperse, and Maria was left alone. Maria continued to berate the on-lookers as they shuffled off after the excitement. One or two remained to commiserate with her. "But the fact is, lady, you do look Semitic." Maria cut this conversation off with a dirty look and walked away.

In my room, Maria's nerves snapped, and she began to cry. It just seemed too hard to struggle against the Germans, against our own people, all ready to sell us out for a couple of zlotys.

We still had no jobs, and our money was running out. But again we set out to find a room for Maria. Our search ended at the home of a Polish sea captain. It was in a safe area, just a block from my own room.

Once her initial rent had been covered, we were really out of money and jobs became crucial. One evening at the end of a fruitless day of following leads in the newspapers, we hopped a tram, glad of a ride home. But just as the tram began to move, the crowds surged and Maria was pushed off balance. As she staggered, her purse came out from under her arm and flew out of the tram into the street. The tram had no doors. Without a thought, Maria leapt off of the back after her purse and her papers. The risks of jumping off the tram were nothing to losing those papers. When the tram finally stopped I pushed my way out and ran back to where Maria had jumped. She was lying on the pavement circled by passersby, bleeding profusely, and clutching her purse. At first it was hard to tell if she was still alive.

I helped her to a nearby pharmacy, where first aid was administered. The pharmacist gave me the name of a doctor. Without any money to pay him, I hesitated. But since I had no idea of the extent of her injuries, there seemed no choice but to go.

The address was in the next street, and with my help Maria limped along to his office. The physician proved to be a very kind elderly gentleman. He examined Maria, took an X ray, and diagnosed a broken bone in her nose and a possible concussion. His prescription called for bed rest.

"I can't do anything about the nose, but don't worry. It will heal."

"I'm sorry, doctor," I apologized, "but we have nothing to pay you with. I promise as soon as we have some . . ." The old man's knowing smile stopped me in midsentence.

"It's quite all right, ladies. Now can I have your address?" He turned to Maria. "I'll want to look in on you in a day or two, with some medicine to hasten your recovery." He must have known who we were and wanted to show how much he cared. I nearly kissed him with gratitude as we left.

We boarded another tram and finally made it to Maria's place. But the captain's wife got one look at her bruised and swollen face and took fright.

"I'm afraid you'll have to go. Right away."

"Please, you can't make her leave in this condition. At least let her stay a couple of days more," I implored through the tears washing down my face. With a look of embarrassment she relented.

"All right, a couple of days."

Maria was very ill. There was no money and no food. I made the rounds of the relief organizations that gave out food to poor and unemployed Poles. I was able to return to Maria's each night with a bit of hot soup and a couple of potatoes. I didn't dare eat them myself. There wasn't enough for two.

One day, in desperation, I went out to wire Frania in Lwów, hoping she could send some money. As I walked back, frightened about the future and hopeless, I was approached by a pair of policemen. They accosted me but I kept walking. One of them caught up and began to keep pace with me.

"What's the matter, you Jewish? You can tell me."

I remained silent, and since he had decided to tag along I changed my destination from Maria's room to my place. Soon enough came the shakedown. But I had no money to give, so he insisted on a visit to my room, just to make sure. By this time, I was indifferent to my fate and I led him there directly. Fortunately the landlady was gone, and the policeman conducted a complete search. Finding nothing, he took my good coat and cut it up, hoping to find gold or jewels hidden in the lining. Finally, in utter disgust, he pulled the watch off my wrist and left. I was left with nothing but his badge number, which eventually I reported to Stach. Oddly enough, my assailant did not seem interested in reporting me to the Gestapo.

I gave myself an hour to regain my equilibrium and left to see my sick friend. I found her worse than before, with a high fever and a bad headache. I didn't have the heart to tell her what had kept me. Soon after I arrived, Maria's physician paid a house call, bringing some medication and an injection. It was only one of several visits for which he never asked payment or information of any kind.

Slowly, Maria began to mend, though her face remained badly swollen. As she began to move about, her landlady became impatient for her departure. At about the same time, the widow boarding me began to make me feel unwelcome and then insisted that she was going to need the space for her niece, who was coming to Warsaw. So we left off looking for work and again turned to finding new lodgings. We combed the neighborhood, asking in the storefronts if there might be a room to let. We gave many in those streets occasion to wonder about the two forlorn young women, one with a black-and-blue face. But no one denounced us as Jews or escapees from the ghetto. In fact, one morning the owner of a barber shop on Rakowieka Street offered Maria his shop to stay in. All he asked was that she come late and leave early, before his help arrived. Maria spent several nights in the shop and was never asked to pay. In fact, the barber found her a permanent place in Mokotow, on the outskirts of the city. It was a fairly safe working-class area. The only problem was that her room was in the same building as the district police headquarters. This proximity proved a blessing, for no one, police or civilian, suspected that the rather Semitic-looking woman who lived in the police precinct building might be on the run.

Our barber, who turned out to be in the resistance, was indeed a guardian angel, watching Maria from a distance. He cautioned Maria not to return to the captain's wife, even though she had left belongings there. Apparently, the police had been by looking for her several days after her departure. They had gotten on to her because the man who had provided the papers turned out to be a double agent. When the underground discovered his game, they shot him. This brought out the police, looking for his customers.

Soon thereafter, our luck turned again. First we received a registered letter from Frania with some money and, more important for Maria, good news. Frania had learned that their nephew Menek had indeed survived the ghetto clearing in Kolomyja. Though wounded in the leg and left for dead by the Germans, he had made his way to the home of a Polish woman who gave him shelter. Mrs. Wojnarowska was a poor peasant woman who, before the war, had done little more than tend the family's houseplants during their vacations. At great risk to herself, this terribly impoverished woman took on the task of hiding a fifteen-year-old in her home without compensation of any kind. Much later we learned from Menek how this righteous Christian woman lived. She survived by boarding Ukrainian boys from nearby villages who were attending school in Kolomyja. Mrs. Wojnarowska had to take the greatest care that these lodgers not learn of Menek's existence. So Menek was never allowed out of the barn. When he contracted pneumonia, she could not send for a physician. She nursed him herself as best she could. Occasionally, in the depth of night, Mrs. Wojnarowska brought him up to her room to give him a chance to warm up. But when dawn approached and her lodgers started to stir, she quickly returned him to the cold barn to hide. But at least he had a chance to survive.

Then it was my turn for good fortune. Screwing up my courage, I reported to the Arbeitsamt (employment office), where I was immediately referred to a German official—Herr Schmidt (pseudonym), Vereidigter Bucherrevision (public accountant—tax examiner for the general government.) His office and home were combined on the same premises and located in the best section of the city, reserved for German offices. My interview was perfectly satisfactory. German was required for the position, so I had to make up a tale to explain how I had come to speak it so well.

"I was a university student before the war. My family is from the east, and when the Russians took over, my father was sent to Siberia and his business confiscated. Then the Germans came and freed us. I haven't been able to find an office job, but I'll be glad to take a domestic position."

The job was mine, along with the title "hausdame." In reality, I was a glorified maid for both the private and the official portions of the establishment. Mr. Schmidt seemed friendly enough, and I was glad to have the job. He was a meek man with a young, attractive wife. His remarks about her suggested that she was having far too good a time in Warsaw and was neglecting their three-year-old child.

My first thought after settling in was how I could contrive to bring Maria to work there. I had to be careful. Just bringing her in as a friend would arouse suspicion. Those sorts of links could carry a chain of friends down when one began to sink.

My employer and his staff were pleased with my hard work. But after the first week, I began to muse mildly about how much work there was to do, what with both the family apartment and office to tend to.

"How about getting a girl to come in and help clean, Mr. Schmidt?"

"Capital idea, Miss Panasiak." And he asked the secretary to telephone the Arbeitsamt that very day.

This had not been part of my plan. I had to act fast. When I got back from the morning marketing later that day, I mentioned to the office secretary that I had met a young woman at a shop who was looking for the very sort of work we had in mind. "Healthy, honest-looking, good references. I asked her to come around tomorrow for an interview." Relieved of the bother of dealing with the Arbeitsamt, the secretary nodded her consent to this arrangement.

That evening, I brought Maria the good news, and we planned our course of action. The scene we played the next afternoon is one I still remember vividly.

It was tea time, a working tea, given by Mr. Schmidt to a circle of German officials, including a Gestapo functionary. I was serving tea while his secretary took notes when the doorbell rang. I opened the door and in came the prospective maid. It was hard to keep a straight face as I ushered her in.

Maria looked the part perfectly; her dress and makeup created just the right image of the peasant-turned-street-girl. She presented herself in the dining room with a kitchen towel in her hands and took a provocative stance. The "peasant girl" couldn't speak any German, of course. She spoke only Polish, and with a heavy working-class accent, one straight from the streets of Mokotow. I served as translator.

Maria drew herself up and looked furtively about the room, her eyes sparkling, but her demeanor showing no sophistication. The assembly began to comment on her in a language they assumed she could not speak.

"She's just too slovenly!"

"But can she do household chores?" asked our employer, ever practical.

I translated into Polish: "They wish to know whether you can work."

"Can I work? Hell, yes. I've spent my whole life on housework."

One of the officers observed: "She looks like a little thief to me."

"Can we trust her in a proper home?" Mr. Schmidt wondered aloud.

"We can try," I said tentatively.

It was the secretary's turn. "Let's look for someone more suitable."

"If you like," I relented. "But let's find someone quickly. The work is really tough for me."

Maria was following all this, of course, but she didn't turn a hair. Suddenly she began to speak in her peasant Polish. "Please, what's the decision? I have to know right away. I got another job offer starting tomorrow. What's the problem? I've worked lots of fancy places, you know—Poles, Jews, even Germans. Lots of good references too. I do windows, laundry, parquet floors, you name it." She stopped and looked at me. "Go ahead, tell 'em."

My employer spoke then. "Tell her to wait in the kitchen, Bronia."

When I sent her out, one of the guests reverted to Maria's doubtful looks. "Did you see her shifty eyes? I'll wager she's a girl of loose morals. She'll bed anyone at all for a couple of zlotys." This made me turn my head demurely.

After some further talk, someone offered: "Why not take her on for a month. See how she does. Meanwhile, you can look for someone more suitable."

I turned to the kitchen, with instructions to give her the job temporarily. With the door safely closed I rushed at Maria and hugged her, choking with laughter.

"What happened out there?"

"Well, they decided you were probably a prostitute and hired you for a one-month trial."

"Let them call me what they want—thief, whore—anything except Jewess."

Maria's performance was rewarded by a job and a room behind the kitchen, the two most crucial prerequisites for survival in Warsaw. But of course, we had to keep our distance from each other day and night. To all appearances, we remained hausdame and maid. I addressed her as "Maria" and she spoke to me in the polite form, but remained the coarse and loud peasant. It was the best cover for her Semitic looks. She even took to carrying the office workers' shirts to her "mother" in Mokotow, who Maria said would launder them at bargain rates. In fact, she took them to the best local laundry and paid the difference out of her own pocket—all to improve her cover story.

In this home and office, we finally settled down to a period of safety and security, the longest and best in all our time on the Aryan side. This family and staff became used to us, hausdame and maid. And it suited us to fade into the background and become part of the surroundings. It was only later that we discovered why the largely Polish staff came to accept us so willingly as part of the community.

As we got to know these men and woman better, we began to suspect that many of them were "ultra-Poles," more Polish than the Poles. They were in fact Jews living, like us, on forged papers and thin disguises. My hunch was finally confirmed when I met one of Mr. Schmidt's new employees. It was a young man I'd known before the war, Bernie Stern. We had grown up in the same town. He had been a fellow student at the law faculty of the Jagiellonian University in Krakow.

Bernie was quite shaken the first time he saw me. All he could do was mutter his Christian name as he passed me, without the slightest outward sign of recognition. I did the same. Later, I shared my discovery with Maria, and we agreed that all parties to this secret knowledge should avoid any further verification of it. Bernie remained Mr. Brezinsky and kept away from the kitchen.

Since I was in charge of preparing lunch for the staff and Maria helped me serve it, we came to know most of them. But we all stayed on our own sides of the professional-domestic borderline.

One of the employees, however, drew our special notice. He had a solid Gentile name, Stelmachowicz, and a relatively senior post as assistant to the director. Nevertheless, his demeanor betrayed him to us as one of our own. Diligent to a fault, he sometimes arrived at the office two hours early, losing himself in his work. He was a bundle of nerves and startled at the slightest unexpected sound. Maria pegged him from the first moment.

Later, when we had become friends, we learned that he had good cause for jitters. Stelmachowicz, or rather Pan Mieczyslaw, had escaped from the extermination camp at Treblinka. He had arrived there in a truck convoy full of people who knew exactly what to expect. As the victims undressed before entering the gas chambers, they threw their clothes into the trucks they'd come in. Stelmachowicz managed to hide himself beneath a large pile of clothes. The guards were on the lookout for this trick and one of them got onto the truck with a pitchfork, spearing the pile several times. Stelmachowicz was wounded badly in the leg. But he muffled his cry and was not found. Late that night, he crawled out of the truck and took to the nearby woods. Hiding by day, he made his way back to Warsaw and found temporary refuge in the home of Gentile friends.

It was a long time before he unburdened himself to us. Though he lived in constant fear of discovery, somehow he sensed that I was Jewish and took to helping me in little ways. Sometimes he took my broom or rag and did a bit of my job, giving me a brief rest. But he lived in fear of Maria. Perhaps her disguise was too good, but to him she really was a low-class Pole, likely to turn him in without hesitation. Her Polish slang and barnyard epithets, her persistent demand that he hand over his shirts for her mother's laundry in Mokotow had him utterly convinced. She seemed a great danger to him and to the others in the office, including me. He even took steps to protect me from her!

Sometimes the office received scarce supplies of food; at other times, we were told that provisions could be secured at warehouses in the city. On these occasions, Stelmachowicz insisted that Maria leave the premises to collect the special stocks. One day, underground sources issued a warning to stay off the streets. The Germans were planning a roundup of young Poles for transport to forced labor in Germany. On that very morning, Stelmachowicz came into the kitchen and ordered Maria to go out to one of the warehouses near the former ghetto to collect a couple of pails of preserves. This was still an extremely dangerous area, but Maria consented. Her cover required her to show no concern. But I protested loudly.

Stelmachowicz beckoned me out of the kitchen and into his own office.

"It's too dangerous for you to go out today. But what's it to the maid. She's not in any danger." The words had left him shaking. I was just as stunned by his blindness and was tempted to blow Maria's cover then and there. But I couldn't without consulting her. I returned to the kitchen. Maria refused to have herself revealed, especially to someone so stupidly blind.

"Why doesn't the fool use his eyes? It only takes one look at me to suspect I'm Jewish."

"We've got to tell him," I answered. "He's scared of you; it's the fear that's blinding him."

But Maria was adamant. So I went out anyway to get the order. Several months later, we let him in on Maria's secret. And then a closeness developed among the three of us. Eventually he fell in love with the girl he had so desperately feared.

Ludmiła was another employee. She too turned out to be Jewish. Young and beautiful, she'd been an actress in the prewar Polish theater in Warsaw. Educated in Switzerland, Ludmiła's special love was children's theater. She had no objection to scribbling numbers and juggling accounts if she could survive to act again. She was fated, however, to give her life on the barricades, fighting with the home army during the uprising of 1944.

Other members of the Schmidt office family let us know, directly or indirectly, that they too were Jews in hiding. And we were sometimes able to help them in small ways.

The Schmidts retained a second apartment in the building. It was vacant, but as hausdame, I was given the keys. Several times I was able to put it at the disposal of individuals, and even whole families with children, who were in trouble. People from the office knew they could trust us, and they came into the kitchen when they needed something. No one ever said more than necessary, and so ties of friendship and trust developed without words. Sometimes we found small but precious gifts on the kitchen table or on our beds—perfume or a bar of scented soap, hard to get and dear. The accompanying notes moved us to tears. We felt we were no longer domestics in a German household and office, but comrades in a struggle for survival.

Opportunities to help increased when we made contact with Jews in the resistance. They were mainly Bundists, members of the Jewish socialist organization, who had survived the ghetto uprising. Some served as liaisons to those living on forged documents. Others hid refugees in safe homes or watched over Jewish children placed in Polish institutions, orphanages, and private homes. They turned the production of false papers into a science, found new homes for people who had been discovered, supported those whose looks or accent put them at risk in public. They organized partisan units and smuggled weapons and food into the concentration camps whenever possible.

After the fall of the ghetto, we began to meet some of its heroes and heroines and the families of those who had fought to the end. We made lasting friendships with some of these people. Among these was Lodzia, wife of the engineer, Michal Klepfisz, who had been among the uprising's leaders. There was a young woman we knew only as Władka. We were told that she was a courageous courier who smuggled weapons into concentration camps and brought news from the inmates to the outside world. There was Bolek, his wife, Ania, and sister Halina, whose underground activities were dangerous and of utmost importance. There was Henryk, a representative of the Bund group on the Aryan side, a gentleman of distinguished appearance. For security, these people were known to us by first names only. They were a great source of support.

From our friends, we often learned the truth about the war and the world at large. Our underground people listened and communicated with the world, but no one listened to them and their desperate messages. One day, sad news reached our friends from London—on August 12, 1943, after futile attempts to transmit information to the world about the desperate needs of the Jews in Poland, the Bund representative in Great Britain, Schmuel Zygielbojm, took his own life on the steps of the Parliament at Westminster. This news destroyed any illusions about getting help from abroad. As it turned out, Zygielbojm's death, as well as the uprisings in the ghetto, in Vilna, Bialystok, and elsewhere, were all in vain.

We were eager to meet more members of Jewish resistance groups. We followed the news from the fronts through underground leaflets and reading between the lines in the German press. The collapse of the German Sixth Army at Stalingrad on February 2, 1943, began to suggest to us the beginning of the end—a ray of light for those still alive.

Sicily was captured (July–August), then Italy surrendered on September 8. Badoglio replaced Mussolini, the Americans bombed Rome. Events moved so fast that we began to spend every minute free from work sharing bits of news or bending over a clandestine radio listening to the BBC crackling through the shortwave. The penalty of being discovered owning or listening to the radio and news from abroad was death. But in the German section of Warsaw where we lived, house searches were not frequent and we had to take the risk of hearing the truth.

Our own desire to be of service to others less fortunate than us continued throughout. Often it was just to find a temporary refuge for one who'd been turned out or lost his money to the extortionists or his job to a jealous Pole. Once a young mother contacted us. Her eight-year-old had been left at her door unannounced when an older sister guarding the child was arrested by the Gestapo. Could we find a place for the child long enough to allow the mother to locate something permanent? The "referral" came from our friends who knew that we had access to our employer's unoccupied apartment on the floor below. We used it and hid the child there for a few days. At other times, we were asked to carry new documents from one place to another for people waiting to come out into the open. One day, I was asked to carry a message to a particular address. I was told nothing about whom I was to meet or why. I found myself in the large courtyard of Hotel Polsky. A group of people was milling around. I asked one what the crowd was waiting for.

"We're all foreign Jews with passports. We've been stranded here in Warsaw and we're waiting for exit visas. We're going to the United States."

How I envied them. What were the chances of smuggling ourselves into this group? I turned this thought over in my mind as I climbed the stairs to the apartment I'd been sent to.

The door was opened by a young woman. Standing behind her, however, was a Gestapo officer in full uniform. As I began to fall away in a faint, the young woman caught me by the arm. She took my message and sent me away. I never learned whom I had seen—friend or foe.

I was still shaken when I arrived back at the office. I went into the kitchen and told Maria about the foreign Jews I'd seen. Maria laughed off my fantasies about joining them.

"They won't get any further than the nearest extermination camp."
She was right. We soon learned that they had all been gassed at Treblinka. So much for the protection of a passport.

Some months into the routine of the household, I received a telephone call from our old friend and protector from Lwów, Edward. He
had lost his cover and was on the run in Warsaw. We received this
news with horror.

I went to meet him at Three Crosses Square, in front of Gestapo
headquarters. He was a changed man. His exposure had been an inside job. Someone had denounced him to his direct superior, who had
sent for the Gestapo. Edward smelled a rat when his boss called him
in and left by a fire exit as the police were coming in the front door to
arrest him.

The first thing he needed was a Kennkarte and the papers to go with
it. We began to work on this problem, a place, and a job, when disaster struck again. Edward was staying in a second-rate hotel. But after
three years on the Aryan side, he had lost the sense of caution needed
to survive. Instead of keeping out of sight, he went out. Not knowing
the street scene in Warsaw, he was soon set upon by two extortionists,
demanding his money in return for not turning him over to the Gestapo. To his protests that he was a Gentile, they responded, "OK. Let's
just slip into that alley and you can pull down your drawers and prove
it." Shaken, he handed over a sizeable amount of money.

After that incident, he tried to stay off the streets as much as possible. Psychologically, he was broken. After this came a further misfortune. We learned of it from a call from a local hospital. Edward had
been brought in with a broken leg. When we visited we learned the full
story. On his way to an appointment with me, Edward had seen the
two extortionists on his tram, or so he thought. He had jumped off the
back platform while it was at full speed and broken his thigh bone. An
ambulance had been required to get him to the hospital. But he
couldn't stay. It was evident to the nurses and physicians who treated
him that he was Jewish, and they were in a panic about the danger.
Since Maria and I were his only family, the danger Edward was in extended to us as well. Besides, Edward was giving our telephone number to other patients in the hospital, to attendants, and strangers, asking them to call us for him. The staff demanded we take him home, or
else.

Finally, Edward told us to call his German ex-wife, Kate, now working in Tomaszow Mazowiecki. The only result was a bit of money for Edward. So Edward called her himself and Kate came to Warsaw for a few days. When we suggested she come to the hospital, she was horrified.

"I can't be seen in a public place with a Jew! Can't you get him into a private clinic?" It was her only thought on the matter.

"Yes, but it means money."

"Well, you can't look at me. I've got to support myself and our daughter."

"But what about all those valuables you were given for safekeeping by Jews before you left Kolomyja? They'll never need them. Can't you pawn some of that stuff?"

"What are you talking about? I never got anything from anyone in Kolomyja." In a fury, Kate pulled a fox collar off her shoulders. "This is all I can give you. Now, leave me alone." Kate left Warsaw and her husband, an invalid Jew on an open ward. Edward began to feel that the medical personnel were neglecting him. Meanwhile whispers about his visitors, Maria and me, began. We had to transfer him to another city hospital. But how? Through friends in the underground, we found a doctor willing to sign Edward into his hospital and to hide his "mark of Cain" as far as possible. But a month after the transfer, Edward's leg became infected, and the doctor began to talk of amputation before the gangrene spread. We were desperate, and Edward became more and more depressed.

"The only way out is suicide. If this keeps up I'll just drag you down with me." Though he talked this way, he made us visit him daily, despite our work and the danger. If we missed a day or two, Maria or I would get a call from a total stranger Edward had asked to reach us. He took risks with our lives and those of everyone else hiding in Schmidt's office.

"Edward," we implored, "you've got to be more careful."

"How about getting me some poison?" was his only response.

In the end, Edward's case came into the hands of a physician who worked with the Polish underground. Under his ministrations, Edward improved, the prospect of amputation receded, and he was eventually discharged into our care. We were able to find him a room, and slowly he got better.

Help came sometimes from most unexpected quarters. I remember in particular the shoemaker who owned a small shop nearby on the

Three Crosses Square. One day Maria and I ventured in to heel our shoes. As we were waiting at the counter, we glanced around at the other customers. When everyone was gone, the shoemaker turned from his work and looked at us with a twinkle in his eyes.

"Ladies, if you happen to know anyone who needs a place to stay on short notice, send him here. It's safe to spend a night or two in my workshop. No one would ever suspect."

After that, the shoe repair shop became an occasional sanctuary. The cobbler never accepted payment. And one day he told us that his wife had left him because of the danger to which he was exposing his family.

"She loves me and wants me to go on helping. But she's got no stomach for the danger. Can't blame her."

Though Poland is a Catholic country, the church did little to resist the fate of the Jews. Rome maintained a silent complicity, and no priest dared to speak out on the subject. And some, like the priest who tested our catechism that first day in Warsaw, participated in the outrages. I wondered what Jews could expect in the privacy of the confessional, and one Sunday at mass, I decided to find out. As seemingly good Catholics, we went regularly, and at the end of mass that morning I impulsively entered the confessional.

"Father, I'm breaking the law. I'm hiding a Jew." It was as close as I dared get to the truth.

The voice that answered me was young. "It is no sin, my child. In the sight of God it is a good deed."

I left the church with tears in my eyes. How I wished that this view represented the official church position.

But for every one person who helped, thousands made a business of taking Jewish money and then collecting a bounty for Jewish lives. The worst of these were the apartment building caretakers. They used their positions to full advantage. Not only were they charged to maintain police registrations but from their lodges they could see all who came and went. Visitors could be questioned carefully enough to build up a lucrative business in blackmail. Many tenants readily gave up their money at the slightest suspicion.

Though we lived at the Schmidts', Maria and I kept our rooms in town. We had legitimate police registrations for them and wanted the extra security of separating our working and living addresses. Sometimes we spent the night in these rooms. We said that we were work-

ing out of town in restaurants that put us up during the week. The
caretakers bought these stories. But we were still nervous about the
odd night at "home." We felt secure only at the Schmidts'. But even
there an incident could rattle us. The caretaker and his wife had a nose
for Jews and their slight differences in appearances. One day Maria
was down in the courtyard, airing and beating the carpets. The caretaker's wife put her head out of the entry lodge.

"Quiet down out there, Maria. This ain't no Jew-house."

This remark gave us a sleepless night. Did she suspect? Should we
be on our guard? Should we be ready to flee? In the end, we decided
to ignore the incident.

One night when our employers were out of town, Maria and I were
alone in the house with Bolek. We were in the maid's room, sitting
around the radio trying to locate the BBC broadcast. Suddenly, the
front door burst open and in came the Schmidts. There was nothing
to do but hide Bolek beneath Maria's bed for the night. In the morning our fugitive left unnoticed.

A few days later, Bolek came back with a gratifying story. He had
been on an underground team whose job was to eliminate one of the
extortionists working with the Gestapo. Poles, Germans, Ukrainians,
sometimes even Jews, had to be dealt with this way.

One day while marketing at the shop restricted to German clientele,
I spied a young woman lingering over the merchandise in a corner.
One glance at her face and posture told me she was a Jew in trouble. I
approached her casually and spoke. "Follow me."

Outside the store she told me she was without papers. Without asking her why, I took her home. Her name was Mila. After discussing the
situation with Maria we decided to keep her in the maid's room till we
could get her some papers. That night we hid her under the bed. But
toward midnight came the wail of the air raid sirens. The house was
in an uproar as Mr. Schmidt herded everyone down into the cellar.
There was nothing to do but lock Mila up in the hall closet and tell
her to keep still.

With the air raid alarm over, the Schmidts were too wide-awake to
go back to sleep, so we were pressed into service. Suddenly, there came
a knock from the front of the house where Mila was hiding. The family turned in its direction and asked what the noise was. With great
presence of mind, Maria dropped a fine piece of crystal in the bedroom
and everyone's attention turned to the disaster. This gave me the mo-

ment to slip the now-faint Mila out of the closet and back under my bed. Only later did we learn that Mila suffered from asthma and was slowly suffocating in the hall closet.

The next day we got some papers for Mila and passed her on to our friend the shoemaker for a couple of nights. We also found her a position working for a family in the German quarter. But a few weeks later, Mila was back at our doorstep. Despite our warnings, she had begun to go about town with her incomplete Kennkarte. Though we warned her that without signatures and fingerprints it wouldn't provide much protection, she ignored our pleas to stay indoors. She was easy prey for street extortionists and soon gave up all her money. She needed more right way.

"Look out the window. See the two kids across the street. They're waiting for me to come up with more dough."

We became frantic. It wasn't the money. It was our cover she was blowing by bringing these thugs to our door. Ours and a dozen others, for that matter.

"Here," I said, handing her some bills. "Let them know it's German money they're taking, and if they come back they'll be finished."

We resolved never to bring strangers into our safe haven. But it was easier said than done. The need was too great not to take an occasional risk.

By April 1944, we had been in Warsaw almost a year. News from the front was getting better, and from the BBC we learned that the Russians had liberated Kolomyja on March 29, 1944. Our joy ended quickly when we remembered that Kolomyja was Judenrein. No one could come out of the cellars to celebrate the liberation—except Menek. When the German army retreated from Lwów, we could rejoice for Frania, Helen, and little Leszek.

Despite the favorable war news, we continued to try to please our employer. There was no immediate prospect of change in and around Warsaw. But it was difficult to keep them satisfied. Little things, incidents you might otherwise laugh off, sometimes threatened our safety. One afternoon, Maria and I were in the kitchen struggling to produce a cheesecake. The family had planned a dinner party that night for German VIPs, but the wood for the stove was damp and we couldn't get it lit, let alone maintain the even heat a cheesecake needs. I kept blowing on the coals till my lungs gave out, while Mrs. Schmidt lurked around the kitchen demanding we produce the cake. Finally, as the meal approached, I shook the wood in a rage, and the whole cheese-cake fell out of the oven and onto the floor.

As I stood there crying, Maria scraped the whole mess back into the baking dish and returned it to the oven.

"But it's filthy now," I protested through my tears.

"Our people have eaten worse."

As she closed the oven door, an even fire suddenly took hold. Forty minutes later, the cake earned high praise from the company.

Success or failure in such trivial matters could seal our fate. Maria often said that it was my mother's recipe for apple strudel that saved our lives. One day I decided to try to reproduce the recipe. It was an evening in May 1944, and the Schmidts were having a guest to dinner. He was a VIP and ran another of the general government's tax offices in Warsaw. The guest must have enjoyed his dinner very much, for at its end he came into the kitchen and peremptorily announced that he was leaving shortly for home and intended to take me with him to Heidelberg. His family, it seemed, needed a maid. He would arrange the paperwork so I could leave in a week or ten days.

My world collapsed around me in a way I never expected. I would have to leave my only family—Maria, my friends—the world built up out of so many sacrifices. Maria tried to console me as well as hide her own pain and loss.

"Liberation isn't just around the corner. You'll be safer in Germany. No patriotic Poles there. Maybe you'll even find something for me. You've got to think positively. We're going to fight this out to the end."

Before my departure for Germany, we met secretly one Sunday afternoon at the apartment of our friends, Ania and Bolek. Somehow our friends got hold of a bottle of wine to lighten the pains of our good-byes. Not being used to drinking at all, we soon became intoxicated. We left late in the evening to return "home." We boarded a city tram. We had barely sat down when I heard Maria raise her voice while looking belligerently at the passengers.

"I am a Jewess if you want to know; so what of it?"

The people in the tram started to come alive as they looked at her threateningly. At this point, the tram came to a stop and I dragged Maria off, forcing her to run with me. We made it all the way home, taking occasional refuge in hallways to make sure that we were not being followed. That was one more narrow escape.

The next few days were sad for us. I had no possessions to speak of, so there was little need for luggage. All I had were human ties that I could not carry with me. I left with Maria for safekeeping the only treasure I had, a picture of Zygmund and Romek, hoping that it would survive the war. Alas, it was not to be.

I didn't want to think about Germany and what might await me there. I only wanted to think of my impending loss. How would I manage without Maria's smile through the dark moments, without her friendship? I was desolate.

CHAPTER

12

Heidelberg

We reached Heidelberg on a lovely May morning in 1944. I emerged from the railway car looking for my employer. Mr. Binder (pseudonym) walked lightly up the platform to meet me, looking rested and satisfied with his breakfast.

I followed him out of the station and into the charm and beauty of the ancient city of Heidelberg. From the tram window, I could see the twelfth-century castle perched above the city and overlooking the buildings of its famous university. The tram glided out of the old city along the banks of the Neckar. Across the river rose a thickly wooded hillside dotted with elegant villas. A path wound around, following the curves of the river.

My employer noticed the enchantment in my eyes. "That's the Philosophenweg. Surely you've heard of it?" The name seemed perfect to me—contemplative and peaceful, like the path itself. How could those who walked it ever turn into the beasts the German nation had become? My mind could not let go of the question. Others who tramped the path, some long after me, have pondered it as well. Mr. Binder broke in abruptly: "This is our stop." We were in a suburb, facing a mountainous path. His house stood at its end. Spring flowers lined both sides of the steep and narrow lane. I could hear the laughing voices of children from the houses. The blue sky, the aroma of pine, the complete absence of war, tragedy, and martyrdom transported me into an earlier world—full of other paths, flowers, woods, youth, and joy. Suddenly I felt human again.

My employer broke in. "This is our place." As we passed through a gate and into the house, a flock of children rushed into the hall from all directions, lunging at their father, eager for kisses and hugs. Their happiness brought tears to my eyes, pushing my thoughts back to Kolomyja, to the Gestapo thugs tearing babies from their mothers' arms and flinging them against concrete walls. I turned away to hide my pain and hatred.

The greeting quickly gave way to introductions. The lady of the house entered and looked me over. When I had passed the test of youth and health, she smiled and invited me to follow her into the kitchen. To my surprise, there was another woman already at work. She looked up and gave a Polish greeting.

A kindred spirit? Her looks made it obvious that I would not be alone. She too was Jewish, I was sure. Left to ourselves, Cesia quickly filled me in. She'd been in this household for a year. The work had been far too much for her, and her health was broken. Thin and pale, she was to be replaced—and I was her replacement.

"But what will you do?"

"I'll go back to the state employment office. They'll get me another job, or I could go back to Poland. That's probably what I'll do." The door swung open, and the lady of the house came in. "Broni, bring some wood up from the cellar." So, with no chance to recover from my sleepless trip across Poland, I set to work. Thus I was awakened to the fact that I had come for forced labor, not a sanatorium. My head throbbed as I went down the stairs.

It was only after nightfall that I was shown to a place in the cellar, the family air raid shelter, which doubled as my quarters. It was a monkish little cell—Cesia's wooden bed, a table, two chairs, a commode, and a bunk set up for me. In a house of ten rooms, a library full of books, a drawing room filled with antiques resting on Persian carpets, we were relegated to the cellar.

"You can put your things in there," said Cesia, indicating a dresser drawer. One drawer was enough for what I had managed to bring: two dresses, a smock, two aprons, a canary yellow coat, and a single pair of shoes. Cesia noticed the coat. "You'll need something warmer for the winter, and I'd get a pair of clogs to wear around the house. Those shoes are too valuable, and besides, they'll never last."

In the gloom, Cesia and I sat down to finish a conversation begun twelve hours before. She began my introduction to the house. "There's the lady of the house to please, then the six children and a governess. The husband works in Warsaw and comes home rarely." As she continued to fill me in, I felt the tension of one who is to displace another. "There are ten rooms in all, plus the garden to care for, with vegetables and fruit trees. You're responsible for cooking and cleaning, the laundry, including the baby's diapers. They're no fun, I can tell you. After you wash down here, you've got to bring it all out back and hang it on the line. The carpets must be taken out and beaten regularly, and they're heavy.

"There's the furnace to stoke all the time for hot water and heat. You've got to weed the vegetable patch and pick things when they're ripe and ready to be canned. Then you do the canning. There's the chicken coop to clean. You saw the hill coming up to the house? Well, you've got to bring all the food and milk for the family up that path."

My head was swimming, but Cesia wasn't finished.

"As to the cooking, they always eat the same thing for supper, a one-dish meal, sort of a thick soup. But it takes forever to make. You use the lousy vegetables we get in the market, and they have to be cleaned. We save all the garden vegetables for canning. The family figures that the war will last for years, and they want to be prepared. See all the jars, pails, lids, and wax over there?" She pointed across the cellar. As she did so, Cesia let out a groan and doubled up in pain. Between winces she told me it was her gall bladder. "There's nothing to do but wait it out. It'll pass. I've got to finish the laundry anyway."

"No, I'll do it. You lie still." She was in no shape to refuse, and she lay there moaning until she fell into a fitful sleep. I quietly slipped into the laundry and tried to finish up the work. It was 2:00 A.M. when she awoke, feeling better and ready to get back to work.

"It's all done." I smiled. Tears came to us both, hers of thanks and mine of dread at replacing her.

"Do you really want to go back to Poland?" I began detailing the dangers and horrors. "It's been a year since you left. Our countrymen have become expert at sniffing Jews out. It's easier to hide here."

"That doesn't matter. I don't have anything to worry about."

I suddenly realized that Cesia didn't think I was Jewish, so she wasn't about to admit that she was.

I had to break in. "Don't you see? I'm Jewish."

"Oh, what a relief!" And with that she demanded everything I could tell her about the Warsaw ghetto, Warsaw outside the ghetto, and how her family died. There was little I could tell her except in general terms. And after a while we returned to our present situation.

"Cesia, you've got to find something here. Going back is impossible."

"But I can't go on. My kidney, my gall bladder. I must have lost twenty pounds since coming here. It's too hard—the garden, the floors, the washing, the cooking, hauling provisions from the village down there."

"There's no alternative."

"Well, maybe, but you better conserve your strength in this job." With that we turned in for a brief night's sleep.

For the next week I followed Cesia about, learning the duties my new life would require. Up at 5:00 and through at 10:00 or 11:00 at night. After two days, I had become a drone. I was not used to such burdens. Every muscle ached and my brief sleeps were punctuated with nightmares. Though the children, ranging in age from ten years to six months, were not my direct charge, I had their laundry to wash, by hand. The infant's diapers were indeed a curse.

My food ration was that of a forced-labor slave—a small loaf of bread. Stupefied by the ration, I turned to Cesia. "How do you manage on this ration? Do you buy food?"

"Buy food? The pfennigs I get are about enough to buy a couple of cups of coffee a week, if I have the time off. No, I steal." She smiled. "Look, you're the cook, so fill up a bit on the soup you're making. Be sure to eat the best bits before you serve it. I always cut some off the children's portions. They never notice. Sometimes I'll grab a raw egg or even a piece of fruit from the garden if I can get away with it. The family's got a larder full of food, enough to last another five years. But it's kept locked."

(I too was paid a "wage." After the war, the German government refused to provide any restitution for forced laborers like Cesia and me. We had been "paid" for our work.)

Mrs. Binder gave me my white cotton badge with the red letters OST—from the Slavic east—emblazoned on it. Cesia advised me to ignore the regulation that required me to wear it in all public places. "It will keep you off the trams, and you'll be forbidden to enter public buildings. With your faultless German, you don't need to bother with it." I followed her advice and tucked my badge into a bottom drawer.

With Cesia preparing to leave, Mrs. Binder called me in to plan my week's work schedule. She listed all the tasks, asking how much time I would require for each. I answered as accurately as I could, until we reached the laundry schedule.

"And how many men's shirts can you starch and iron in an hour, Broni?" she asked. Having never touched an iron, I had no idea.

"Oh, six or eight." Mrs. Binder's face showed me I'd made a mistake. She had broken into a very satisfied smile. The next morning, as I struggled for over an hour trying to iron one shirt properly, I knew I was in trouble. When she saw the result, she cursed me for being a liar. But we both knew she could not easily replace me. (German women would not work in menial jobs.)

Another week went by and Cesia found herself a situation with a war widow in the old city. So I was left to deal with this family on my own. I had a half-day off each week, plus every other Sunday afternoon. So I took to wandering through the woods up to the old castle above Heidelberg. I walked alone and no one interrupted my sorrowful thoughts. I passed. To the Germans, I was just a Polish domestic, like others they saw every day.

My loneliness was broken occasionally by letters from Maria back in Warsaw. These letters were the high points of my life. In my own letters back, I made light of the work and said nothing of the craving I felt for food. I had no right to complain. I was safe from discovery, free from persecution. Indistinguishable from German women, I could walk the streets and ride the trams, leaving my identity card at home. But between the lines of Maria's letters I could read the dangers of daily life in Warsaw.

An invisible little maid, to whom no attention need be paid, I began to lose my perennial wariness, and my shattered nerves settled. I found myself outrageously happy just not being noticed as I walked through the town or the footpaths in the forest around it. It was a feeling I had not known since before the war. After a time, I even found myself going to sleep at night without fear of an "Action," and the nightmares died down. Here in Germany, as long as I continued to do my work well, I had the freedom I lacked in my own country.

With my employer I was correct but distant. I told her little about myself and tried to keep my "story" uncomplicated and believable. "You speak such fine German," she observed.

"Yes, my family is ethnic German."

"But you speak in such an educated way."

"Well, I was at the university briefly before the war."

"What about your family?"

"The Russians took them. They were all sent to Siberia. I'm all alone. It was a miraculous escape."

"Then you're not used to this sort of life."

"But I've got to support myself. I'm grateful for the chance to work as a housemaid. Besides, my mother trained me well in household duties."

After our first few talks, Mrs. Binder decided she would have to treat me rather differently from a housemaid. To begin with, I was offered the run of the library. I declined. Then she began to confide in me.

"Oh, Broni, the miseries this war has produced. And all this misfortune brought down on us by the damn Jews."

I seethed. But sometimes it was hard not to break out in hysterical laughter. One day I was informed that the "know-nothing" Jew, Einstein, had swindled the theory of relativity out of an Aryan scientist. This and other tidbits came hot off the presses of the *Sturmer;* this family accepted without question all exhortations to live up to the Führer's standards.

Mrs. Binder had married young, but had been unable to conceive a child for eight years. "It was inflamed ovaries. They operated on me, and I lost one. But with the other I've produced seven children for the fatherland, and the eighth is on the way. Our Führer expects nothing less."

Patriotic education started early in the family. The seven-year-old girl was already a member of the Pimpf, a children's organization. I would hear her after school practicing the slogans members had to learn, full of venomous abuse of Jews and Slavs. *Jude* was a scare word around the house: "Behave yourself or the Jew will get you." Even the eight-month-old boy responded to it.

One afternoon, Mrs. Binder came into the kitchen and invited me to share some coffee and conversation. As an educated woman, she wanted to learn more about Poland, before the war and now.

"Tell me, Broni, have you ever seen an Ostjude? I haven't, but my husband has told me about them. Ugly, dirty, hairy half-animals. You must have seen them in Warsaw."

"Well, yes." I looked at her with perplexity. "But they all looked pretty much like us. Except maybe for the Orthodox, who had beards."

"No, that can't be."

I was not about to argue, but in a tone of honest inquiry I replied: "Have you ever seen a Jew here in Heidelberg?"

"Of course. We had lots of Jews, mostly scientists and professors, some lawyers and doctors. But that's different. And even though they had no right to exist at all, we allowed them all to go to America years ago."

As Cesia had foretold, work in this house was more than any one person could handle. Like her, I began to lose weight and had to resort to theft. I began by fishing out the best parts of the soups and stews that I made for the family, then I began filching food from the pantry, the cellar, and the garden. The fruit trees were full, but my hausfrau kept a careful count on what was ripe.

"Broni, there were five peaches on that branch yesterday. What happened to them?"

"I have no idea." She shot me a look of disbelief.

For protein, I had the chicken coop. As I cleaned it or fed the chickens, I reached under a hen and grabbed an egg, cracked it in my hand, and swallowed it raw. Unlike the fruit trees, the chickens never gave me away.

When things became really tight later in the war, I managed to copy the larder key and steal a jar or two of the preserves we'd put up. I'd save it until Sunday afternoon and clean it out with a spoon or fingers as I walked the woods with Cesia, and later with Maria.

Survival in this household took ingenuity as well as industry. Some jobs were just impossible without it. We bought whatever was available from the village grocers. On one occasion it was a large bag of unhusked kidney beans. To shell each individually would be impossible. I had a day's work to do besides making supper. Tears came to my eyes as I looked at the bag of red beans. There had to be a way to do this job faster. I picked up the twenty-pound sack and carried it out into the yard. There I set it on a workbench and spread out the beans. After covering them with a cloth, I began to beat the beans with a mallet. After a few strokes, I examined the results. Sure enough, I was being covered with a fine red dust, but the hulls were coming off. To improve efficiency I went into the house and up to the couple's bedroom, where I found a hairdryer. Back down in the yard I plugged it in. The blast of wind carried the dust and shells away as I beat. I had the job done in an hour, at the cost of a day's wheezing and sneezing the dust out of my nose and throat.

May passed into June and then July and August. The war news from the west made little impression, but then came news about the home army's uprising in Warsaw. The Russians had reached the Vistula and occupied the suburb of Praga. In the city, Poles, including some of my friends, were fighting for liberation. And here I was, a thousand miles behind enemy lines. My spirits soared anyway. My hausfrau became more anxious with each passing day.

"Broni, have you heard about the atrocities? They're actually attacking our people on the streets of Warsaw."

I began to worry about Maria, caught in the crossfire. Her letters stopped. I was convinced she had joined the resistance. Then, on October 2, the German radio announced that the Wehrmacht had reoccupied the city.

We got a firsthand report when Mr. Binder came home for a brief holiday. Asking too many questions could betray me, but I had to take the risk.

"Did you see the Schmidt family in Warsaw or any of the staff in his office?"

"Why, yes." He looked up. "Remember that beautiful girl who used to work there? Ludmiła was her name. Turned out to be a vicious terrorist, joined the underground and started killing German soldiers. But she got it in the end. Riddled with bullets when the Wehrmacht regained control."

I was staggered. I remembered Ludmiła well, the lovely actress so eager for liberation and the chance to return to the stage. Her words came back to me: "Don't worry, the Germans will go to hell, and I'll head for the nearest show." At least she died with a couple of German lives to her credit. That was the best epitaph my thoughts could give her.

Mr. Binder had no news of Maria. I would not bring myself to think of her as gone too. She had to survive. My last hope could not be destroyed.

Mr. Binder returned to Warsaw, and life went on. My aimless walks and tram rides sometimes took me down into the city, where I visited Cesia. I was glad to see her in a less-demanding job, one that enabled her to regain some of her health. For her sake and mine, I was glad she'd decided to stay in Germany.

One day in the fall, my wanderings brought me to the ancient buildings of the university. I strolled down the halls, reading the notices. As it turned out, there were lectures on literature open to the public on Thursday afternoons—my half-day off. How wonderful, I thought, if I could spend a few hours here, freeing my mind from the aching body it inhabited.

Thursday came, and I hurried through my morning chores, hoping against hope that I might soon find myself in a lecture hall, just perhaps with a handful of "freethinkers," Germans who had not sold their souls to the Reich. I was to have a rude awakening.

The large hall was already packed as I slipped in. As the lecturer approached the dias, everyone rose, and he was greeted with the united shriek, "Heil Hitler."

Our speaker's topic was "the influence of the Niebelungen on German literature and music." The Niebelungen is a Germanic epic myth of the early thirteenth century depicting the ideas of fate and loyalty to the chief. It includes many pagan legends and traditions. The poem ends with general slaughter and holocaust. The lecturer began with a long political discourse and then turned to the ideas of "fire" and "the fire gods" in German myth—the apotheosis and inspiration of all-consuming fire. The image brought me back to the horror-stricken eyes of the ghetto, the elderly Orthodox huddled together intoning the Shma Israel as their synagogue burned above them, with young Nazis throwing bundles of books on them, shouting their hatred of the poets, thinkers, and scientists who had made German culture great. I was awakened from a vision of the burning Reichstag by the lecturer's peroration and the frenzied chorus of "Heil Hitler." The audience moved toward the exits, carrying me along. So this was the character of intellectual life in modern Germany. I came out into the street thinking, "Are they all murderers?"

Weeks later, I met the first person whom I could call "righteous." He was a physician the Binders consulted occasionally when a child became sick. At one point when he visited the house, he must have noticed my accent, for he asked me where I was from. I told him that I was Polish. I soon won his trust, and he confided his story. He had once been on the faculty of the university. He was dismissed from his position when the industrious bureaucrats discovered that his wife was half, maybe a quarter or even an eighth, Jewish. He had been given a choice of divorcing his wife or leaving his position; he chose the latter. He opened a private practice, but was shunned by all "right-thinking" people. His reputation as a diagnostician was so good, however, that he was still consulted on occasion, though discreetly. By the time I met him, his wife had been sent to Theresienstadt. She was not to survive the war.

Despite my initial experience at the university, I continued to attend lectures on my Thursday afternoons off. As I rushed through my work on these days, my hausfrau looked at me quizzically. I think she must have suspected that there was a man in my life.

One Thursday the subject was Rainer Maria Rilke, whom the Nazi culture had embraced. I had learned many of his poems by heart long before the war. I settled down to enjoy hearing them again and to think about their meanings. As I tried to be inconspicuous in the last row, my eyes wandered over the backs and heads of the other listeners. Mrs. Binder, what was she doing here? She must have followed me. Why? What was I to tell her? I could no longer focus on the lecture. I slipped out of the row as quietly as possible and headed home, hoping she had not seen me. Perhaps she'd just chanced to walk in herself?

The next morning as I was preparing breakfast, Mrs. Binder came into the kitchen.

"Broni, I saw you in a lecture hall at the university yesterday. What were you doing there? Nothing of interest to a maid or a peasant girl in Rilke. Who are you anyway?"

"I told you, I had a bit of university before the war." It was hard to sound cool and unemotional in the face of discovery. "It's nice to spend my free time improving myself. It makes my work go better." For a change I'd told the truth, though fiction and fact about my own life were so jumbled together that I had not noticed. Somehow she accepted my story and dropped the matter. But I decided it was just too much of a risk; I'd have to stop going. Instead I began to explore the trails through the forest, searching for peace in the solitude of the pines along the Philosophenweg and the farmland beyond Heidelberg. Sometimes I came to the old castle above the river valley and occasionally caught the music of Haydn or Mozart wafting out of the windows of its great hall. I remember listening to the "Ode to Joy" from Beethoven's Ninth Symphony.

I came to know the narrow cobblestoned lanes of the old city better and better. I stopped at each historic marker, read it carefully, and learned much about the history of the city. I remember one engraved tablet fixed to the side of a building along the Neckar:

Heidelberg! Oh Du Feine
Du Stadt am Ehren Reich
Am Rhine und am Maine
Kommt keine stadt Dir gleich

Hidden in the woods close to home, I chanced upon an enchanting little coffeehouse. I visited there on my Sundays off. With the few pfennig I had, I bought a cup of imitation coffee and a few hours of escape from my reality.

One morning in November 1944, after having received no word from Warsaw in months, Mrs. Binder's voice interrupted my work beating the dust out of the large carpets.

"Broni, there's a letter for you." My heart began to pound. Trying to stay calm, I told myself that it was probably a mistake. I couldn't risk hoping. A few moments later I was holding a crumpled postcard in my hand. It bore Maria's handwriting. I left my work and hurried to the basement to read her card alone, slowly and repeatedly, until I had learned it by heart. I felt as though someone had reached out from the dead and touched me. Maria had been wounded in the fighting and because of certain "circumstances," wanted to come to Heidelberg as soon as possible. Of course, I understood what the "circumstances" were well enough, but I was overjoyed at her survival. Nothing else seemed to matter. But how could I bring her to Heidelberg?

The return address was Poste Restante, Tomaszow Mazowiecki, a city near Warsaw. I wrote back immediately, though I knew that "circumstances" would keep her on the move. Then I began to think about getting her a work permit to travel to Germany. After some inquiries, I found that one of our neighbors needed a new maid. They were quite insistent that she be a "professional maid, strong and in good health." There was housework, gardening, laundry, and more.

"She's quite strong and capable," I assured them, knowing nothing about her current condition. So, the family filled out the papers, and I sent them off to the only address I had. There was nothing to do but hope she would be able to get back to the post office and be able to use the documents in time. I knew Maria was a fighter, and I clutched this knowledge as my only hope for her.

A week passed, and I began watching for the mailman. As he came up the path I would intercept him. I feared that one of the children might get to the mail first and destroy my letter. After another day of waiting in vain for mail, the nine-year-old came to the top of the cellar stairs.

"Broni, there's a beggar woman at the gate. Says she knows you, but I don't believe it, she's so ragged. She says her name is Maria." I rushed up the stairs and around to the front of the house. There was Maria, a kerchief on her head and a bundle in her hand, smiling happily, as if to say, "Here I am."

The joy I felt as I hugged her and carried her down to my room in the cellar! After a moment I had to tear myself from her side and return to my work. Mrs. Binder noticed the stranger and asked what she was doing there.

"It's all right, she's the new maid for our neighbors. She starts tomorrow. Can she stay the night? She'll be no trouble."

"Yes, I suppose so."

When nightfall came, I was ready to explode with questions. We sat down on the bunks and shared my food ration. "Tell me everything that's happened since I left Warsaw."

Maria caught her breath and began. "The first couple of weeks after you left were rough. The Schmidts didn't replace you, so I ended up doing everything. I tried to stay in touch with the underground and visited Edward every chance I got. Everyone was beginning to feel hopeful, because it looked like the tide had finally turned against the Nazis. The Red Army was getting closer every day, and when one of Rokossovski's units reached the Vistula at Praga, the Polish Resistance Forces challenged the German occupation. They took up arms on August 1, 1944. The Warsaw uprising began in hopes of speeding the withdrawal of German forces from Warsaw. The fighting went on for two months, but on October 2, the Polish Resistance Forces surrendered. The Russian forces remained inactive on the banks of the Vistula in the suburbs of Praga.

"But what about you? How did you get out?"

"In the end, when we knew things were hopeless, we emerged from the sewers into the bank of the river. A lot of people came down trying to get across to the Soviets. That was our only hope. I came down with Bolek and Halina. There were a couple of small boats and a tremendous crowd, all trying to get on. We tied a rope between us as we pushed our way to the boats. There was this terrific glare from reflectors the Germans set up to light up the river. Artillery shells started coming down around the boats halfway across. Many people drowned.

"We tried to stay together, but it didn't work. Bolek managed to get to a boat, and I think he got away. Then I was hit. Halina was holding me tight, and I was shot in the back. The bullet went right through me and into Halina's arm. In the crush, we didn't even notice it. But then, the bleeding got much worse, and I lost consciousness. I must have been out for quite a while. Suddenly, we were surrounded by German soldiers and marched into the unknown. We were joined by many others. The city was on fire. We were forced to carry a white sheet as a symbol of surrender. We were choked by smoke, and I cannot remember how long we were on this march. We were all brought to Pruszków assembly camp. I was terribly thirsty and my wound kept bleeding. I was half-conscious and cannot remember just when it was that we were brought to a railway station and pushed into a train. Halina was with me. We were with fighters with torn military uniforms. Someone mentioned that we were being taken to the Pruszków labor camp. At dawn, one of the Poles sitting across from us said to the other one: "These two girls look Jewish." Halina and I knew then that we would be denounced before the train reached its destination. As the two men dozed off, Halina and I looked at the window and decided to jump.

"I cannot remember what followed except that I was awakened in the house of a Polish woman who told us that a priest had found us in the field and, noting that we were still breathing, brought us to her home in Tomaszow Mazowiecki. He assumed we were Polish fighters in the Warsaw uprising. The Polish woman treated us with much awe and admiration as if we were heroines. She shared her food generously with us, though she was evidently poor. She tried to patch up my wound and was eager for details about the Warsaw uprising.

"We knew that we could not carry on this facade of being Poles for too long. As soon as she recovered, Halina left. A day or two later, a neighbor came in and our hostess proudly introduced me to him, bragging about my patriotic role in the Warsaw uprising. Without commenting, he followed her into the kitchen and said that I looked Jewish. My heart stopped. The next morning, the woman suggested that I leave. There was no discussion. She put a half a loaf of bread and two apples into a kerchief and saw me through the door with her blessings. These were my only possessions, except for the coat with the bullet hole.

"As I found my way into the city, I spotted a pharmacy, and since I felt I had nothing to lose, I walked in and asked for employment. The owner was pleased to hear my story of the Warsaw uprising and offered me a job. I was to wash apothecary bottles and assist with other chores. He was so enthusiastic about helping a Polish woman from Warsaw that he sent me to his wife for food and lodging for the night. It was that night that I sent the card to you.

"I cannot begin to tell you how marvelous it felt to sleep in a clean bed and to be able to wash up. Somehow, I felt secure with this family and with the prospect of a job. However, the following morning the pharmacist's wife told me—with much apology—that I would have to leave. I was sure that she had identified me as a Jew. Believe it or not, this was not the case. With embarrassment, she told me that they found lice in my bed. When she learned of the infected wound in my back, she suggested that I go to the city hospital to have it cleaned and treated. I went to the emergency room, where a doctor attended to my injury. In the midst of terrible pain, as he cleaned the wound without anesthesia, I heard his assisting nurse tell the doctor that I looked Jewish. I walked out to the street, totally resigned, homeless and hopeless. That night, I fell asleep on a street bench, but was awakened suddenly by a German soldier who told me to follow him. He brought me to a public bath for delousing. The place was filled with other Polish women, some vagrants and prostitutes. After our clothes were disinfected we were marched off to the railway station and put on a train with a destination of a labor camp in Germany.

"The train stopped in Katowice, Silesia, a town on the German border. The foreman brought us to a corner at the station, telling us that the next train to Germany would leave in the evening. We were not to leave the station.

"German soup kitchens had been set up at the station for ethnic Germans escaping the Russian front. They dished out some food for us too.

"I had earlier caught whispers about me among some of the Polish women and knew that it was just a matter of time before someone would turn me in. In the commotion of the crowded railway station, I sneaked out into the street. A brown shirt (Nazi elite) parade was marching through town. I joined the march, even the salute to Hitler. Later in the evening, when I was sure that the transport I was supposed to be on had left, I returned to the railway station.

"That's when I decided I would have to get to you in Heidelberg. It took several weeks getting on and off trains, eating at the refugee soup kitchens (identifying myself as ethnic German). Mostly I traveled at night. During the day I hid, usually in ditches or woods, sometimes in public toilets. I remember one day while in a toilet, I saw a woman who really gave me a fright. There she was, leering at me, black skin, half crazy. Blanca, it was me, looking in a mirror. All that soot and coal dust. I had to look three times to be sure it was me.

"Now, I look almost presentable. But best of all, I'm here. If you are not a mirage then this is the luckiest day I've seen in a long time."

Maria's wound still oozed and that night I heated up enough water for a bath. As I cleaned her wound I began to worry. How would she be able to report as fit for work as a maid in the neighbor's household tomorrow? I voiced my fear, but she reassured me. "Let's worry about that tomorrow, OK?"

From the time Maria came to Heidelberg, time passed much faster and far less painfully. To begin with, we had each other, and this made every burden lighter. True we still had to work hard keeping our employers happy, but when evening came we took comfort from each other's presence, sometimes in contented silence. We managed to get the same days off and took to strolling the wooded paths I had discovered earlier. Sometimes we ended up at the castle, listening to an open-air concert and holding hands like a pair of lost but happy children.

We had lost contact with the east and could only hope that Edward was safe. Maria could merely report that he had been hospitalized in a small town to the south.

We tried to read between the lines of the German news. But increasingly this was unnecessary. The news reports could no longer hide German losses and withdrawals. The winter of 1944 was our fourth of the war. We had survived long enough to begin to hope that we would see the victory. While the airwaves and the posters on the walls still extolled the inevitable victory, the offensive in the Ardennes began and failed. The German people remained confident, but we became more so.

That winter I became ill. It began as an infection on my upper lip, but soon I began running a high fever. I was taken to the medical clinic for foreign workers and found myself lying among a multitude of sick and dying in an annex of the university hospital. The food was skimpy and so was the medical attention. Eventually I was transferred to a civilian ward, where I was given proper treatment. In my delirium

I began swearing that I was a Jew and that I was condemned for abandoning my child. Maria sat by my bed and struggled to calm me. Sometimes she simply had to cover my mouth to stifle my screams. But Maria had to work and could not stay with me continually. Fortunately, most of what I said was in Polish.

That Christmas in the hospital was especially sad for me. The Hitler Youth was active on the ward, preparing a Christmas party for the patients. In my delirium I did not want to die among Germans, who would only look upon me with the contempt they held for "Polish trash." What was I doing here, they would wonder, taking up space that a German could use? The murmuring was beginning to drive the will to live out of me. On Christmas day Maria came, with a gift from my employers. Generosity was quite out of character with them, and I could only see the present of a few hand-me-downs as the desire to secure the friendship of the Untermenschen, the slaves and foreign workers. With the war going badly, they must have been thinking about the aftermath.

That Christmas day, I was discharged from the hospital. The next day, in Maria's attic garret, Maria and I celebrated our birthdays (both on December 26) with imaginary wine, toasting the coming Allied victory.

Nineteen forty-five began badly. This time Maria fell ill. It was a leg fracture, caused by a fall on the attic stairs. There was nothing she could do but lie still for weeks. Her employers decided to keep her at home. The war was coming close in western Germany and they felt she'd be better off there. As she lay recuperating, the German radio finally began giving clear news about the situation on the war fronts: retreat from Belgium, from Lodz and Krakow. Then Warsaw, Silesia, a separate peace removing Hungary from the Axis. "But we will astonish the world, still," the radio commentators shrieked. We counted the days to freedom.

As Patton's Third Army pushed toward nearby Mannheim we began to hear the sounds of war again, but as a symphony of liberation. Still, it had its ironies and dangers. One morning, the air raid sirens sounded. I was climbing the path from the shops below, carrying food and pails of milk. Then I saw the planes, American fighters coming in low. I was out in the open. There was nowhere to take cover, so I hurled myself to the ground and rolled over to the hedges. How silly, after all this, to be killed by an Allied bullet; it was almost funny. As I rose, I realized that in my rush for cover I had knocked over the milk pails. It seemed a small price to pay, but Mrs. Binder did not think so. She carried on for days about the spilt milk. I should have expected no less. Whenever I broke something, she would insist it was an "irreplaceable heirloom."

As the air raids grew more frequent, I found myself sharing my cellar with the Binders. Mrs. Binder awakened me rudely, ordering me to give my cot to the children and stand for the duration of the night. I couldn't really regret it, considering the cause.

With liberation literally over the horizon, Maria and I began to think about getting across the front to the approaching Americans. But Mannheim was a German stronghold. So we probably couldn't have succeeded, but we thought about it constantly.

While the radio barked its warning about the new "miracle weapons," all we ever saw were deserters flitting through the woods fleeing the front. Some would come out into the village, begging for civilian clothes. They were turned away with abuse for their defection.

The collapse brought with it a new threat to us. We knew that the Nazis were making every effort to efface their atrocities by killing as many as were left in the camps and driving the foreign workers together for speedy elimination. We learned of this through leaflets dropped in the woods, urging all foreign workers to avoid such roundups and save ourselves. Maria and I decided to declare ourselves Volksdeutsche—ethnic Germans. We approached our employers with this tale. They accepted it readily. After all, as Volksdeutsche we would not be subject to any roundup, and they would not lose their servants. Moreover, they might also place us in their debt after the Allied victory. We were duly registered with the authorities and left alone.

There was another ruse I played in the final days of the Third Reich that gave me a little satisfaction. The impending doom produced hysterical fears. My employers feared for their property, not their lives. It was rumored that the Americans would confiscate everything of value, especially antiques. So we set about hiding the most valuable pieces. I was ordered to dig a hole in the garden, to store china, crystal, gold, even food and clothing. With each spadeful of earth I turned, I felt myself burying the thousand-year Reich.

At times Mrs. Binder was consumed by the thought that the Russians would receive this part of Germany for occupation. One evening she approached me in a state of great anxiety. "Broni, you've lived under the Soviets. How did you manage it? What was it like?"

"Oh, Mrs. Binder, it was horrible. You can't imagine." And I proceeded to describe every depredation I had ever known the Nazis to commit, only substituting Soviet for German.

"But that's unbelievable. What will become of my family, my children?" She decided to prepare enough poison for herself and the children should the Soviets approach.

Recalling the fervent hope of so many ghetto mothers to poison themselves and their children, I asked: "But Mrs. Binder, what if you poison the children and then find it was unnecessary? Will you still kill yourself?"

"Ach, no. I'd still be young enough to have more, for the Führer and the fatherland!"

In March, Germany was in flames. "Bombenterror" they called it, a new method of warfare they invented, though nothing compared to their other atrocities. The Soviets had four million soldiers in Prussia, the U.S Third Division was on the Rhine and in the Saar. Then the Ninth Division crossed the bridge at Remagen. The appeals and the threats to the German nation from the Führer's bunker persisted. But no one could credit the claims that victory would still be won.

About March 20, we learned of Eisenhower's call upon the citizens of Frankfurt and Mannheim to evacuate their cities for their own safety. In Heidelberg the German authorities appealed to the very old and young Germans to join the "Volkssturm," or the "werewolves" fighting behind Allied lines. But Mannheim fell to the Ninth U.S. Infantry Division a day later. The next morning Heidelberg was gripped in fear, awaiting the Americans. Suddenly, the air raid sirens went off. What could it mean? Oblivious to any danger I rushed out of the house and onto the path.

"They want to clear the streets, so that a delegation from the city can meet the entering Americans and assure them of cooperation." But in fact nothing happened that day, for the city officials apparently could not agree on how to proceed.

The next morning I was still at work scrubbing the kitchen floor when Maria rushed in.

"Get rid of that brush, throw away your broom. Come on, the Americans are marching through the village!"

For a moment I couldn't move. All I could do was absorb her words. Then I rose. Soon I was hurtling down the mountain path in my wooden clogs. Behind me I heard the voice of my hausfrau.

"Hey, where are you going? Come right back here, Broni. I'll report you to the Arbeitsamt."

I stopped in my tracks, laughing. "It's finished! My day has arrived, and yours is over!" By this time Maria was tugging at me.

"Come on, don't bother with her."

As we reached the road we could see the khaki-clad soldiers, some in tanks and some on foot, some young, others old, some tired, others curious, staring out from under their helmets at the two "German girls" embracing, crying, laughing in uncontainable happiness.

But the ecstasy was short-lived. Throughout the war years, we had had two all-encompassing aims: to survive and to see Nazism in ruins. On this Good Friday, April 1, 1945—two years to the day since Maria and I had landed in that police station in Warsaw—our promise and our hopes were fulfilled. The Nazis were defeated, and the lives we had fought for so very hard were secure at last. But what were they worth? We had no families, no homes, no future—only an unbearable past. As if for the first time, our minds became fully open to the ghetto pictures and smells accumulated over so many years: of unmarked graves; of air rancid with the smell of decomposing bodies; of suffocated, mutilated, martyred children. How would we ever live with the memories and the guilt? Full of these thoughts, questions, and fears, we greeted our first moments of liberation.

13

Aftermath

As we sat by the side of the road, our despair overcame the exhilaration of relief. Troops marched by and an American officer detached himself from the column and approached us. He seemed curious about our tears. He spoke in English, but to no avail. We, in turn, tried German, Polish, Russian, and French. Nothing seemed to work. Then his eyes brightened, and out came a few words of Yiddish: "Are you girls Jewish?" Astonished, we nodded.

Somehow he made us understand that he was a chaplain in the United States Army, and we were the very first Jewish survivors he had met. He could not stay, but he scribbled his name and told us to come see him at the Heidelberg city hall, the American headquarters.

After he left, we began following the troops into the center of town. Heidelberg had been surrendered quietly in the end, and there was no destruction. As we slowly walked through town, we realized that we were still in considerable danger. Even though we were on the American side of the front, there was still a war going on, and no immediate sign of German capitulation. (In fact the war in Europe did not end officially for a full month.) The Ninth Division was only passing through. It would leave at most a small occupation force in control of the city. We might as well have been in no-man's-land. Fearful of returning to our employers, we went to the home where Cesia worked. She took us in for the night. The widow for whom she worked seemed only too eager to be helpful, now that the war was over.

The next morning, we presented ourselves at the city hall and asked for the chaplain. He had already gone, but he had left word that we were expected. The officer in charge promised to try to find something for us as soon as possible.

As we left, Maria asked: "Well, what shall we do?"

"I don't know. I suppose we'll have to go back to Cesia's cellar."

"Not me," replied Maria firmly. "I'm going back to my employer's place. I slaved there for six months; now they can put me up for a couple of days! Then I'm going to see the village administrator and requisition a nice little apartment for myself."

I was aghast. "Maria the place is lousy with Nazis. You'll be easy prey. It's not worth it."

"No, it will be worth it. I just want to see Herr Doktor and his Frau put up with their ex-maid and a Jewess to boot in their Aryan home for a while. Besides, they'll have to protect me. They need us now. There's going to be no better friend to have in occupied Germany than a Jew."

Maria turned out to be right.

That spring, freed from slavery, we spent long hours every day tramping the Philosophenweg, though a curfew required us to be in by dark. As the occupation authority promised, within a few days I was assigned a studio apartment in the old city. Now, with roofs over our heads, the problems of food and money became paramount. German girls had no qualms about fraternization, but we could not bring ourselves to reach our hands out for chocolate bars, C rations, and Spam. After years as slaves, we would not beg. So we had to line up at the soup kitchen set up outside the city hospital.

Whenever we approached the occupation authority officers, we were at the mercy of the translators, Germans with no interest in passing our requests on to American officers. Despite a half dozen languages between us, neither Maria nor I could actually communicate with our liberators.

In our wanderings through the city one day, we came upon a new poster. The American authorities were sponsoring a meeting for all surviving Jews. The meeting was to be held at a house behind the sight of the burned-out shell of the synagogue of Heidelberg.

On the meeting day we set out eagerly, asking each passerby to direct us to the sight of the old synagogue. They looked at us blankly.

"Huh? There's no old synagogue in Heidelberg."

"Yes, yes, but the ruins, do you know where they are?"

In the end, a small boy pointed the way. "There's a playground there now," he explained.

A group of relatively young people had already gathered. Only a few knew each other. We began by introducing ourselves in little groups. Some, like us, had survived on false identity papers. Others came from labor camps. There were maids and factory workers, and every so often we heard a cry of joy or disbelief. Strangers instantly became friends. People embraced, kissed each other, or just held hands tightly. I stood in the middle picking up scraps of conversation.

"I don't believe it, Friedrich, you're not Jewish! Why, I've worked next to you for two years in fear that you might turn me in."

"Turn you in? You looked so utterly goyish, and you always seemed to be looking at me suspiciously."

The meeting had been organized by a young American rabbi. Moved to tears, he told us that we were the first Jewish survivors he had met. In the next few weeks he took it upon himself to help each of us find shelter, food, work, and the means to pick up our lives. His advice to everyone was "learn English." So I invited a young German woman who spoke the language to move into my flat and employed her to do nothing but speak English to me. It was "total immersion." In a few days, I could begin a rudimentary conversation. Maria progressed as well.

But Maria continued to cause me anxiety. One morning she came to town from her employers' home with a bit of a story.

"Last night Herr Doktor dropped in on me. He told me I'd have to leave. He said that his wife couldn't keep house and they'd have to get a new maid, so they were going to need my room."

"You should have gotten out of there weeks ago," I observed.

"I said to him, 'Sure, I'll be glad to go, as soon as the administrator finds me the flat I asked for.' Then he changed the subject. 'Maria,' he said, 'what are you and your friend Broni going to do now that the war's over? Go back to Poland?'"

"'No,' I said, 'not yet anyway. We're going to stay here a while and rest. It's very beautiful, and we've got years of war to recover from.'

"Then he says, 'Well, I guess you're in no great hurry to get back to Poland anyway. You'll have a lot of explaining to do about your time here in Germany. First you were Poles, then Volksdeutsche. The Soviet occupation forces will have some tough questions for you.'

"That was too much. I stared him down and told him we had nothing to fear from the Soviets. We weren't fascist Poles or ethnic Germans. 'We're Jews, you fool, and we'll be honored by the antifascist forces back in Poland for surviving your war.'"

I was surprised. "You mean you hadn't told them yet, and they hadn't figured it out?"

"From the look on Herr Doktor's face, no, they hadn't. But he sure started singing a different tune. Right away he says, 'Funny, all along I thought you were Jewish. That's why we kept you on you know, to protect you.' I said to him, 'Why if you'd known we were Jewish we wouldn't have survived a day.' 'No, no,' he says, 'I swear.' Then the floodgates opened and he began going on and on about all the Jewish doctors he'd saved, smuggling them over to Switzerland. Anyway, I couldn't stand it, so I finally threw him out."

"But when are you going to leave?" I asked.

"Blanca, I'm not going to leave. My boss ended up saying I could stay until I got my own place. As if he could stop me. When he left I felt so great I wanted to come right down and tell you the whole story, but what with the curfew, I had to stay put. I wish you'd been there. The revenge was sweet. Only the Germans have a word for it, *Schadenfreude*."

Soon after that, Maria and I got some work—in a USO club for GIs, mainly waiting on tables and frying up the doughnuts that the soldiers loved. We ate our fill and began putting on weight. Most important, we began to learn more and more of their language, the living language of Americans, not the stilted textbook English of my German tutor. In fact I began to learn words that could not even be found in a dictionary. Without fully knowing their meaning I began to spice my conversation with *damn* and *hell* and far worse.

One afternoon, I was using my English with an officer. After a few sentences he stopped me. "Where did you learn to speak English like that?" he asked.

"Right here, from the soldiers."

"Well, you speak pretty well, but you can't use that kind of barnyard language. Ladies don't use those words. Get it?" Soon enough, to my embarrassment, I understood.

Learning English was the most important thing to me just after the war. Everything depended on it. As I got better, I was promoted to better jobs, ones that involved more and more English. Within a week of becoming a waitress, I graduated to the information booth at the recreation center. To do my job well, I memorized a half dozen short speeches. I chose one on the basis of what words I could recognize in a question, even when I didn't really understand what was being asked. So, whenever I heard the word *mess hall* I'd give my set speech about directions on how to get there, opening times, and so on.

One afternoon, an officer approached and asked for directions. What he said sounded like "mess hall," so I gave him my set spiel. The officer looked astonished, and I began to wonder what I'd done wrong.

"What languages do you speak?" he asked.

I took the question for "what language are you speaking?" I answered: "Why English of course."

The officer could see I didn't understand. "I mean, besides English."

I mentioned three others, but we could find no other common ground. Finally, like the chaplain, he tried a little Yiddish. That worked, and he told me that what he had wanted was directions to the castle, not the mess hall. He left laughing. "You'll learn English fast, my dear, since you have enough chutzpa to work behind the information counter when you don't even speak the language."

A few minutes later he returned. "Say, instead of seeing the castle, I think I'd like to spend some time with you. Can I take you out or something?" So, we spent the rest of the afternoon in a cafe, where, through broken Yiddish and English, I told this young officer of my war experience. He left Heidelberg later that day, saddened. "We must never let what happened be forgotten." It had already become a motto.

A month later I was hired by UNRRA—the United Nations Relief and Rehabilitation Administration. The director in Heidelberg was a Canadian Jew, David Wodlinger. He treated Maria, Cesia, and me with the greatest courtesy, but he was eager to learn everything he could about what had happened. After working in his office for a time, Wodlinger got Maria and me jobs, first at the UNRRA headquarters in Frankfurt-am-Main, and later at the American Joint Distribution Committee in the UNRRA building—an office requisitioned from I. G. Farben. The man in charge, Jacob Trobe, told us we were the first European Jewish employees they had.

When the war finally ended on May 9, we still had no direct knowledge of the suffering in the camps and labor factories. Now, as people trickled into Frankfurt, we began to learn the grim details. Joint, as it was known, ran a displaced persons—DP—camp in Salzheim near Frankfurt-Hochst. There we tried to supply life's necessities. Since we spoke several languages, Maria and I went to the camps daily and began to meet newly liberated survivors as they came into the camp from all over Germany. Mostly they wanted to know if other family members had made it. They kept asking questions. I was doing the same, looking for someone, anyone, from my home town of Gorlice. I had to find out about my brothers, the twins. I had lost contact with them early, when they were sent to the labor camp in Płaszów. Finally, one man told me about a boy he'd been with in a concentration camp who said he was from Gorlice.

"Is he here? Can you find him?"

"Yes, I think so." I followed him through the camp, till he led me up to a youth of eighteen, who looked at me suspiciously.

I looked back. It was my cousin, Josef Korzenik, Paula Bergman's brother. "It's your cousin, Blanca," I said smiling. He collapsed in my arms crying. I couldn't expect him to recognize me, for he had been only six when I married and left Gorlice. He was there still when the Germans came and the Actions began. He knew everything about how my family met their fates. He told me each person's story.

"What about Bernie and Izak?" I asked, interrupting his account.

"The last time I saw them, we were all being herded into a vast hall. Then they began the selection. Mothers and children to the left, males to the right. I was holding onto my father's hand. Your brothers were holding hands with their father—your father. When the Germans started their selection, separating older from younger men, our fathers, yours and mine, pushed us away and toward a group of young people destined for labor camps. We were all sent out that very day. It was the last time I saw your brothers. We left in separate transports.

"But I heard what happened to them later. They made it through the first three years in labor camps. They were sent to different camps, but finally ended up in Krakow-Płaszów camp. It was just a week or ten days before the end when the SS cleared the camps and started driving all the inmates west to get away from the Soviets. They drove them days and nights mercilessly, no food, no water. Anybody who fell or tripped was just shot. That's what happened to your brothers. I heard it from eyewitnesses."

My twin brothers. They were only eighteen years old and they came so close to survival. We brought Joe to visit with us in Hochst. He was my family, perhaps the only one left. Joe had survived through six different camps. We wanted to know everything and we questioned him closely. He shared the horrors he and others had suffered and seen. For his part, Joe wanted to learn everything he could about our lives. After listening to them, he observed: "But you're heroines."

"Why do you say that, Joe?" I replied. "What happened to us is nothing compared to your experiences in the camps."

"No. Don't you see? We knew where we were and what would happen to us. As long as we could work, we'd survive, and when we couldn't, we'd be killed. That was it. It was simple. You were out here, fighting for survival, surrounded by enemies, alone, always looking over your shoulder, never knowing where the next threat would come from." I didn't argue.

"I remember the day when at work I managed to get hold of a couple of rotten old potatoes. When I got back to the barracks that night, the guard made me strip, and so he found them. He beat me senseless . . . and for two rotten potatoes."

These stories preyed on my mind when I would hear German civilians proclaim utter ignorance of the extermination camps. Our landlady was one. Her husband had been a medical officer in one of the camps and was now interned by the American authorities. Loudly she proclaimed that she'd never heard anything about them, though her husband came home every weekend.

Our jobs at UNRRA and then Joint brought us in touch with the flood of homeless people wandering aimlessly from place to place across every frontier in central Europe. It was the young people who touched us the most. All we could do was meet their material needs, for the wounds were too deep to reach. Though the war was over, many continued to deny they were Jewish, even at the cost of support from Joint. They had learned their lesson too well.

Once the UNRRA Tracing Office was organized, we spent much of our time with refugees, going through long lists in efforts to find relations and especially to reunite parents and children. Mostly all we could do was record information and add to the lists—name after name, and so rarely a reunion. We matched people from the same town or even region, scrupulously recording every name they could remember. But there was little we could offer beyond vague hopes.

One day, two girls from Gorlice came into the office. Though we'd grown up in the same town, I hadn't known either of them.

"Did you ever know my brothers, Bernie and Izak?" I asked.

"Yes, we worked with them for about a year at Krakow-Płaszów. But then they were sent to Skarzyska."

"Wait," the second girl added, "I remember someone telling me that they made it and survived." This news brought the conflict of hope and despair I'd seen in so many others directly to me.

A few days later, a newly arrived DP from the east told me he'd seen my husband, Wolf, in Katowice, back in Poland. I couldn't rely on these reports, but I knew I would have to go back to Poland to learn what I could for myself. Perhaps a remnant of my family had survived. Maria too had learned something about her surviving family. Her sister Frania and Frania's son Leszek had been cited as survivors. We both decided we'd have to go back. It would be difficult. We had no documents. The borders were still sealed. There were zones of occupation to cross and no travel orders to procure rail tickets anyway.

We discussed the problem with our boss at Joint, Jacob Trobe.

"Don't go," he pleaded. "It's too risky. As soon as they open the borders and things get settled down, we'll help you. But it's too soon."

"No, we've got to go now." Maria and I were adamant. "The trail gets fainter every day."

We gave up our jobs, prepared to go, and said our good-byes. Trobe gave us letters of introduction, requesting Joint officers throughout Germany to give us their full cooperation on our trip to Poland. And we got it. Right across Germany, we had lodging and transport, food and shelter. From Frankfurt to Munich, we were to head for Regensburg, on the Czech border. There were three of us, for we had brought Joe along to search for his sister. At Regensburg, we would have to cross the frontier through the woods at night. When we got to Munich we were warned that it would be dangerous. Both the German and Czech border patrols had taken to shooting people going in either direction. In Munich we met the leaders of groups bringing Jews out of Poland to Palestine. They urged us to wait a few weeks, but we wouldn't listen.

At the Munich station, waiting for the train to pull out for Regensburg, I began to worry. What if we didn't make it across or got trapped on the other side? I turned to Maria.

"Look, it's silly for us both to go. We're not being smart. If one of us stays behind and the other gets into trouble, the one at Joint in Frankfurt will be able to help. I'll go on. You go back and I'll find Frania and Leszek for you." It took a lot of convincing, but finally Maria consented. We parted once more, for the third time. Through the tears and hugs she pulled off her coat and began struggling with its hem. Out came the wrinkled hundred-dollar bill she'd been saving since before she left Warsaw in the fall of 1944. It was to be my bankroll in Soviet-occupied Poland.

The train whistle sounded and Joe and I climbed aboard. We got to Regensburg a few hours later and met the guide who would lead us across the border.

It was after midnight when we arrived at the crossing point. The guide led the way. We could hear the sound of gunfire around us. Soon he urged us to run. Several in our party dropped their bags to keep up, but after a while the guide slowed down, smiled, and said, "Welcome to Czechoslovakia." We made our way to a border train station and climbed aboard a train to Prague.

In Prague I made my way to the Joint office, where my letter of introduction secured me lodging, food, and help on the next leg of my journey. There was a day's wait before heading for Poland, so I took in as much of the city as I could.

I had never been to Prague before, though Wolf had studied there and told me much about its beauty. I wanted to explore it as a free woman, not as Bronislava Panasiak. The first thing to do was rid myself of my carefully cultivated "Aryan appearance." I walked into a beauty salon and told the young Czech hairdresser to cut off the long blond braids I had crowned around my head like a Bavarian peasant. The girl spoke Czech and I Polish, but we managed to understand each other. We could just as well have spoken German, a language we had in common, but neither of us had a taste for it any longer.

"Such beautiful blond hair. Why do you want to get rid of it?"

Briefly I recounted my history. Tears filled her eyes but her work continued. When she had finished, I looked in the mirror and saw a new woman entirely.

"How much?"

"Please, it was my great pleasure and privilege. You are the first Jewish survivor I've met. I can't accept anything."

I left her feeling we were united by more than just a common hatred of all things German.

The next day, Joe and I left for Katowice, armed with visiting documents provided by Joint. The morning we arrived we made for the

Jewish survivors' committee and asked for the Kolomyja register. The only name on the list I recognized was that of a colleague of Wolf's, a Dr. Stern. But he was listed under an address in Gdynia, a port town on the Baltic, hundreds of miles to the north. The only thing for me to do was go. It would be dangerous, and I'd have to wait two days for a ticket and a seat on the train, but there was no choice. Even the carriage roofs had no "vacancies."

I took a room to wait out the two days before I could board my train. The next morning, as I walked back to the Jewish committee, once again I noticed a tall man in a Russian uniform. As we got closer I saw that it was Wolf, my husband, headed to the same office with the same object: to find me.

Our meeting was restrained. Our conversation was forced and almost cold. I shuddered at the emptiness I felt as we exchanged greetings after four years apart. We stood a few feet apart, looking each other over, not touching or crying, just looking. Finally I spoke: "Let's go up to my hotel."

As we walked, Wolf began speaking. "Blanca, what of our son?" Suddenly, I felt accused. I broke down. "He's where most of our children have gone." Now I understood the gulf between us. On my side, the feeling of desertion, betrayal, abandonment; on his, guilt, the need to justify, to explain. Yet he began by accusing me. Why had I survived and not his son? As I sobbed, he began to make idle conversation. I hated him.

Later we talked. Wolf was in Prussia with the Soviet Field Hospital. He had known for some time that I had survived. There were rumors that I was somewhere in Germany. "I wanted to find you," he explained, "but I just didn't know how to go about it."

I remained silent.

"I have the afternoon off; let's go out to Gleivitz." It was a small town nearby.

"Why Gleivitz?"

"Oh, I forgot to tell you, Sam's living there. You remember, Samuel Rosenberg."

The name resounded through my head like a thunderclap. Here was my husband, with me for the first time in four years, eager to lead me back to a past I had forced myself to repress, to forget. The very mention of the name brought back those long-dormant emotions, now perhaps too strong to resist.

We drove out to Gleivitz. It was an emotional reunion. All three of us exchanged details, people we'd lost or found, heroes, and villains. Sam drained me of anything I could tell him of his wife and daughter. Then they talked about their war, Siberia for Wolf, Stalingrad for Sam.

After a time Wolf got around to a girl, a Russian girl he cared for very much. He had hoped to get her out of Russia and bring her to Poland. Grasping at straws now that he had a wife again, he turned to Sam.

"Could you marry her and bring her to Poland?"

Though he proclaimed continued devotion, I could see what was in Wolf's mind and heart. Hearing about his girl in Moscow was all I could take. Our married life had been brief and seemed so long ago. The war years had changed everything. I had paid a terrible price for my survival. No parents, no brothers, no child—not one relation closer than a second cousin. It was, I thought, time for me to build a new life on the shattered remnants of the old. Now, at last, I felt truly free and knew that it was time to give Wolf his freedom as well.

"There's no getting back for us," I said. "Let us go our separate ways." Wolf seemed sad, but it seemed to me also relieved.

A few days later, I went to Krakow and found Frania and Leszek. It was a warm and emotional reunion. The absent Maria dominated our thoughts. They told me that Menek too had survived and was now working in Lwów. After Krakow I went to Lodz to see my friend Lodzia Klepfisz. My mission complete, I got back to Gleivitz, to Sam, and began to plan my return to Frankfurt and Joint. I knew my native land no longer had anything to offer me. I made my plans to get out, but Joe wanted me to go with him to our hometown, Gorlice.

"You've got to come with me. It was your home. Your grandparents left their houses and factory there. You're the only one left. You have to claim what is yours. I heard that your grandparents buried gold, jewelry, and money in the ground on the premises of the factory. It's yours now if you find it."

"No, for me Gorlice is just a cemetery without headstones." I cared nothing for the empty houses and ghost-haunted factory. I had no desire to say Kaddish for my dear ones in that place. "Go, Joe, find your sister. I'm going back west."

The next day I set out. But this time I was not alone; Sam rode next to me. We had no words left, but the warm grasp of his hand on mine was a comfort. Slowly the train inched away from the wreckage of all that we had known and into an unimaginable future.

Epilogue

These war memoirs were written primarily to be a private legacy to my children, Mark and Alex, and my grandchildren, Eugene and Adrianne. But during the long hours and days of writing, I felt first a strong resurgence of my mourning and then the beginning of a healing process. Part of that healing was due to my husband Sam's never-failing understanding, support, and encouragement.

Sam and I married in Salzburg at the end of 1945. Our twin sons, Mark and Alex, were born there. In April 1949 we emigrated to the United States on a visa sponsored by the American Joint Distribution Committee. Such visas were issued to a number of Jewish physicians who had no relatives to sponsor them.

Our early days in the new country were difficult. The boys were two and a half years old. Although Sam did not speak English, his sponsors required him to start work right away. We were supported for the first year in New York by NYANA, the New York Association for New Americans. Sam was to begin internship immediately at the New York Jewish Memorial Hospital. He earned fifty dollars per month, and a meager supplement came from NYANA. I had to be a magician to make ends meet. Since I could not go to work because of child care, we took in a boarder and "sublet" our couch in the living room. The additional ten dollars per week was a great help. At the end of that first year, our support from NYANA stopped, and Sam was told that he had to accept a post as a physician in a state psychiatric hospital in Spencer, West Virginia. The job was a blessing, in that it would provide immediately for our housing and other essential living expenses. Sam accepted the position with regret, since our lack of money made it impossible for him to complete the required two years of residency in his specialty—gynecology and obstetrics—a field he loved and for which he was gifted.

In the summer of 1952, we left Spencer and moved to Cedar Grove, New Jersey, where Sam took a position as psychiatrist at Overbrook Psychiatric Hospital. One year later we returned to New York, where Sam passed the New York State Medical Board exam and obtained his license. He then was offered a position as a psychiatrist with the Veterans Administration. He stayed there until his retirement in 1973.

In the fall of 1953, I entered Columbia University School of Social Work and completed my graduate training in 1955. After graduation, a new life unfolded for me. I loved my profession, and in it I found a new meaning to life and a new sense of myself. To help other struggling people meant a lot to me. I had thirty-five good years of professional life. For twenty years I was an educator on the faculty of my alma mater.

I have never ceased to remember all those who helped me survive the Holocaust years. First and foremost is my dear friend Maria Rosenbloom, to whom I refer as my "alter ego." Maria emigrated to the United States in 1947. She worked for the American Joint Distribution Committee and soon received a fellowship that enabled her to enter Adelphi School of Social Work for graduate studies. She was in the school's first graduating class in 1952. Several newspapers wrote stories about this brilliant student and war survivor. Maria devoted her whole life to the service of others and to education. She became a professor at Hunter School of Social Work and taught generations of students for about thirty years. During the last fifteen of those years, she originated and developed a curriculum for teaching a graduate-level course on the Holocaust. Jewish and non-Jewish students enrolled in her class. Maria was a superb teacher, highly respected and honored. At the time of her retirement, the Hunter School of Social Work created a Holocaust library in the name of Maria Hirsh Rosenbloom (Najder), thus honoring the first and only Holocaust teacher on the faculty of that school.

Maria and I remain very close friends. We are joined by ties stronger than blood.

Maria's close family who survived the Holocaust years were her older sister Frania Gitterman and her two nephews, Menek Goldstein and Alex (Leszek) Gitterman. All these became a "family" to me in the postwar years. They continue to take me into their midst, offering love and care, just as they did in the days of the ghetto in Kolomyja. Frania's son, miraculously saved from the flames of the Holocaust, became known affectionately in my family as "Big Alex," to differentiate him from our son Alex. Later, "Big Alex" became a professor and then dean of Columbia University School of Social Work.

Maria's older nephew, Menek Goldstein, our other "ghetto child," survived the war in Mrs. Wajnarowska's barn on the outskirts of Kolomyja. After the war, Menek found his aunts Frania and Maria in Europe and a new life seemed to await him. Health problems caused him some setbacks. When he was about to board the ship in Bremerhaven to join his aunts in New York, he experienced a hemorrhage and ended up spending several years recuperating from tuberculosis in a Swiss sanitorium. As he got better, he enrolled at the University of Bern and earned a doctorate in biochemistry. Eventually he came to the United States and became a distinguished professor at New York University. Several years ago, he received an honorary degree in medicine from Karolynski Institute in Sweden.

Menek never forgot the Polish woman who saved his life. He supported her through the years and when she died, he memorialized her in Yad Vashem in Jerusalem, planting a tree in her name in the Avenue of Righteous Christians. I was privileged to be invited to that unforgettable and moving ceremony.

Of the many others who were of importance in my life, I pay special tribute to Lydia, the director of the ghetto factory. It was she who provided me with the false identity papers and offered all the help I needed to make my escape from the ghetto possible. In spite of many attempts, I have never been able to connect with her in Kolomyja after the war. She will always remain a heroine in my thoughts and heart. The other friend, our one-time "cross to bear" was Edward, or "Mr. Glac." He survived, remarried, and lived in Israel for a number of years before he died of a heart attack in the midsixties.

Pan Stelmachowicz, our forever-anxious office manager in the Warsaw household, did not fare as well. After his miraculous escape from the extermination camp at Treblinka, he died of a massive heart attack shortly after the war.

Of the several friends that Maria and I met in the Warsaw underground, the one who remained the closest to us is Lodzia (Rose) Klepfisz, the widow of Michal, one of the heroes of the Warsaw ghetto uprising. Lodzia was lucky to have been able to rescue her only child, Irena, who stayed in a Christian orphanage in Warsaw throughout the war. Shortly thereafter, Lodzia and her daughter left Poland for Sweden and later for the United States. After years of struggle, Lodzia became an archivist at the American Joint Distribution Committee offices in New York. She has been most helpful to many writers. Irena became a fine poet, writer, and champion of women's rights. Mindful of her Yiddish heritage, she became a teacher and lecturer on Yiddish themes at several universities in the United States and abroad. Her father was posthumously awarded a medal of Virtuti Militari by the socialist Polish regime. One of Irena's most memorable poems reflects her search for her father's body in the wreckage of the Warsaw ghetto.

Mila, the desperate Jewish girl I met on the streets of Warsaw and hid in the closet, survived the war. She made her home in Sweden.

David Wodlinger, our Canadian friend and first boss at UNRAA in Heidelberg, married a Jewish war survivor. He and his wife live in California, and we keep in touch. I remember with special fondness his efforts to fatten us up after our hungry years in Heidelberg.

I want to pay special tribute to Cesia Osenton, the maid in the German household in Heidelberg. Shortly after the war, she married an American serviceman and made her home in Tacoma, Washington. She has kept in touch through letters and wonderfully chosen gifts to our sons.

My cousin Joe Korzenik came to the United States on a visa he received from his paternal relatives. That child survivor married a lovely American girl and settled in Hartford, Connecticut. We are in close touch. His sister Paula was lucky to be reunited with her husband, who survived in Auschwitz. They live in Israel.

Of those few Poles who helped us, I remember with special appreciation Stach, the policeman who set us free and saved us from the Gestapo, the corner shoemaker who offered help to "our kind," and the physician who took care of Maria after her accident on the tram in Warsaw. Each of these people provided a glimmer of light in the darkness.

My wonderful marriage of forty-two years came to a sad end with Sam's death on December 28, 1987. We had good years together in spite of our many early struggles. As I look back now, all the experiences stay with me and bring me peace.

As our two sons were growing up they brought us a great deal of joy. Both became fine young men and have found happiness in the lives they have chosen. Alex is a professor of philosophy and chair of his department at the University of California at Riverside. He is a prolific writer and speaker, and he carries our name with pride and distinction. He and his wife, Merle, have given us two wonderful grandchildren. Mark's life has taken a less-traditional course. He has become a disciple of Yoga and lives part of the time in South India. He is currently working on his doctorate in comparative religion at the University of Virginia, Charlottesville. He is a talented and loving man. Both of our sons are close to me. My only regret is that they live so far away.

My story is now complete. Preparing it has been difficult but also critical for my own healing. Now Romek's legacy is fulfilled at last. May it serve the cause of peace.

Index

28 **DATE DUE** *Rays*

GAYLORD | | | PRINTED IN U.S.A.